HOW TO BE AN EXTREMELY REFORM JEW

DAVID M. BADER

Illustrated by Jeff Moores

AVON BOOKS ◢◣ NEW YORK

HOW TO BE AN EXTREMELY REFORM JEW is an original publication of Avon Books. This work has never before appeared in book form.

AVON BOOKS
A division of
The Hearst Corporation
1350 Avenue of the Americas
New York, New York 10019

Copyright © 1994 by David M. Bader
Illustrations copyright © 1994 by Avon Books
Illustrations by Jeff Moores
Published by arrangement with the author
Library of Congress Catalog Card Number: 93-49849
ISBN: 0-380-77599-9

Library of Congress Cataloging in Publication Data:

Bader, David M.
   How to be an extremely reform Jew / David M. Bader.
      p.   cm.
   1. Jewish wit and humor. 2. Jews—Humor. 3. Judaism—Humor. I. Title
PN6231.J5B23   1993   93-49849
808.88'2'089924—dc20   CIP

First Avon Books Trade Printing: September 1994

AVON TRADEMARK REG. U.S. PAT. OFF. AND IN OTHER COUNTRIES, MARCA REGISTRADA, HECHO EN U.S.A.

Printed in the U.S.A.

ARC   10   9   8   7   6   5   4   3   2   1

CONTENTS

AUTHOR'S NOTE

In writing this book, I set out to build a gateway to a deeper understanding of the Jewish faith, to shed light on the historic and religious character of Judaism, to show how rituals and practices relate to concepts at the core of Judaism. When these goals proved way beyond my reach, I went for a few cheap jokes instead. *How to Be an Extremely Reform Jew* is not, however, an attack upon Judaism. Its purpose is merely to enable Extremely Reform Jews to laugh at themselves and their peculiar approach to religious observance. Its aim is to reach, but not to preach—to teach, but not to beseech—to bleach, but not to peach. (For more of this, see my previous book, *The Extremely Reform Rhyming Dictionary.*)

There are those who will complain that *How to Be an Extremely Reform Jew* is not a substitute for thoroughly studying the Five Books of Moses, the Prophets, the Writings, the Talmud, the various restatements of Jewish law, and the many commentaries on continuing halakhic questions. This is true, but anyone who tries that approach will end up missing a lot of good television.

For guidance through the intricacies and nuances of Judaism, I thank the Archbishop of Canterbury, who provided some excellent pointers. I also thank my agent, Lisa Bankoff, and my editors, Bob Mecoy and Lisa Wager, for their indispensable help, as well as Amy B. Miller, Joseph M. Doloboff, and, of course, the Rosenbergs (Ben and Karen, not Julius and Ethel). I am especially appreciative of the thoughtful suggestions received from my family, most notably, "Why don't you *do* something with your life?"

I grudgingly admit that, in covering a 4,000-year-old tradition in 96 pages, I possibly may have left out some things. I accept all blame for any mistakes and feel very guilty about them already.

David M. Bader

INTRODUCTION

What Is an Extremely Reform Jew? If you're not quite sure, you might be one. "Not being quite sure" is a cornerstone of Extremely Reform Judaism, as is "not really knowing," "not having a clue," and "not having any kind of an attention span whatsoever." Extremely Reform Judaism is one of the fastest-growing religious denominations in the world, although its exact size is difficult to measure because no Extremely Reform Jew has ever actually shown up for a meeting.

This movement in Judaism goes far beyond the Orthodox, Reform, and Conservative debate over how to interpret and follow biblical laws. The Extremely Reform Jew, instead, asks a more contemporary question: "Laws . . . you mean there are laws?" While other Jews ask of religious rituals,

TRADITIONAL AND EXTREMELY REFORM JEWS: SOME BASIC DIFFERENCES

Traditional Jews	Extremely Reform Jews
Believe their form of Jewish worship is the only truly authentic form of Jewish worship.	Believe their failure to attend services is the only truly authentic form of failing to attend services.
Will marry only within own faith.	Will intermarry only within the major world religions.
Believe the Five Books of Moses were written by Moses himself.	Believe the whole Bible was written by James Michener.
Give children biblical names.	Think Ashley *is* a biblical name.

1

"Does this make sense?" the Extremely Reform Jew instead asks, "Does what make sense?" Indeed, at a time when other denominations are struggling to reconcile Jewish traditions with the demands of modern society, Extremely Reform Jews have fashioned a practical, socially relevant compromise: "I'm really busy right now. Let's discuss this some other time."

Extremely Reform Jews are often treated with suspicion, if not outright hostility, by those who deplore their seeming lack of interest in religion. Extremely Reform Jews have tried to correct this false impression, pointing out that it was an Extremely Reform Jew who first posed the question: "Why *can't* we have a Christmas tree?" Whatever the truth may be, other Jews routinely denounce Extremely Reform Jews as "secular Jews," "three-day Jews," "non-observant Jews," and, most cuttingly of all, "Extremely Reform poopheads." This intolerance is saddening because Extremely Reform Jews have many complimentary things to say to their more religious brethren (e.g."Nice *yarmulke!*"). Indeed, Extremely Reform Jews have much in common with Jews of all denominations, as well as with several types of Episcopalians. The point is, whatever our differences, all Jews are related, if not quite as closely as the population of the Ozarks.

WHO ARE THE EXTREMELY REFORM JEWS?

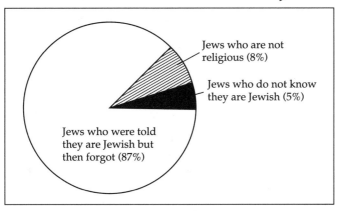

Jews who are not religious (8%)

Jews who do not know they are Jewish (5%)

Jews who were told they are Jewish but then forgot (87%)

1.

FROM ANCIENT MESOPOTAMIA TO ENGLEWOOD, NEW JERSEY:
The Extremely Reform Story of a People

Extremely Reform Judaism first arose among the shepherds and nomads of the ancient Fertile Crescent, who worshipped idols and ritually sacrificed sheep, oxen, and an occasional close relative. Unlike other ancient peoples, however, the forebears of Extremely Reform Judaism were not very religious and, if pressed, described themselves as idol-worshippers, "but only in a cultural sense." In around 2000 B.C., the Prophet Abraham persuaded his followers to abandon idol-worship altogether by telling them that "God is one" and that "monotheism saves time." Abraham's followers became known collectively as the Hebrews, even though none of the Extremely Reform Hebrews could actually speak the language. They were also called the Chosen People because of their special "covenant" or pact with God: If they worshipped Him, He would give them all the Land of Canaan and any furniture that came with it.

The most important figure in Extremely Reform Judaism after Abraham was Moses, an Extremely Reform Prophet, who was born to Hebrew parents but then raised as an Egyptian. Archaeologists believe that he probably would have gone on to marry a WASP had any existed at the time. It was Moses who led the Jews out of slavery in Egypt and into the desert, where he gave them the Ten Commandments. (The Eleventh Commandment—"Find water!"—is no longer in effect.) Extremely Reform Jews maintain that they were not really "Commandments" at all but just "Suggestions," and that Moses looked very dehydrated when he delivered them.

After receiving the Commandments, the Jews spent forty years wan-

THE TEN SUGGESTIONS

1. I am the Lord thy God and thou shalt have not too many other Gods besides Me.

2. Thou shalt make no graven images. This is a major religion, not a shop class.

3. Thou shalt not take the name of Adonai thy God in vain without the express written consent of Adonai thy God. The name "Adonai thy God" is the sole property of Adonai thy God. Any use of the name of Adonai thy God without the express written consent of Adonai thy God is unauthorized and illegal and shall be punished by Adonai thy God.

4. Remember the Sabbath, thy squash game, and thy other appointments.

5. Honor thy single parent.

6. Thou shalt not kill a man just to watch him die.

7. Thou shalt not commit adultery and then run for office.

8. Thou shalt not steal. (Note: Not really applicable to car radios.)

9. Thou shalt not bear false witness against thy neighbor when appearing before Judge Wapner.

10. Thou shalt not covet thy neighbor's wife, his servants, his flocks, or his power tools.

dering in the desert, somehow managing to miss all the oil fields. Some of these Jews were Extremely Reform, while others were simply Extremely Stubborn About Asking for Directions. Archaeological excavations indicate that when King Solomon was finally able to build the famous "First Temple" in Jerusalem, he had great difficulty getting Extremely Reform Jews to show up for services.

In 586 B.C., the Babylonians destroyed the First Temple, explaining afterward that "it had been just too damned long since anything terrible had happened to the Jews." The calamity forced the Jews to spend years reconstructing the Temple, and every service had to begin with the prayer:

O God, Creator of the Universe, Ruler of All Things,
please pardon our appearance while we renovate.

When it was finally completed, critics raved that the Second Temple was just as good as, if not better than, the First, not unlike *Godfather II*. Excavations from this period indicate that Extremely Reform Jews still did not attend services.

> **"If I forget thee,
> O Jerusalem, send me a note
> or a reminder or something."**
>
> —*The Extremely Reform
> Book of Psalms*

When the Second Temple was destroyed by the Romans in A.D. 70, many Jews began to feel that, what with the crumbling infrastructure and high crucifixion rate, ancient Jerusalem was not the city it used to be. Thus began the "Diaspora," a Greek term meaning "migration to countries where everyone hates you."

For hundreds of years, wherever they went, Extremely Reform Jews

---

THE TALMUD

While some Jews ran for their lives, others stayed in the Holy Land and wrote a comprehensive code of Jewish law, the Talmud. This task took centuries, hindered by persecution, writer's cramp, and a running debate over whether the Talmud should prohibit snacks between meals.

Why did generations of Jewish scholars consecrate their lives to Talmudic study? Possibly, the endorsements. ("A long day of circular reasoning can give a great sage a terrible headache. That's why Rabbi Joshua gives his blessing to Talmudic Strength Excedrin.") It took rabbis 300 years to compile the Jerusalem Talmud and 200 more to finish the Babylonian Talmud. Extremely Reform rabbis have spent the last thousand years trying to sell the movie rights.

were legally barred from entering most guilds and professions except money-lending, and were not permitted to own land except in Venice, Italy, where they were not permitted to own water. In France, they were forcibly baptized and ordered to adopt the metric system. In England, the nobility confiscated their wealth to pay for the Crusades and required them to serve as live targets during archery practice.

The Spanish Inquisition was particularly infamous for brutally persecuting people caught practicing Judaism, except for Extremely Reform Jews, who were brutally persecuted for "being Jewish in a cultural sense." To avoid persecution, many became "Secret Jews," practicing their faith covertly behind a facade of conformity. The Secret Extremely Reform Jews of Spain bravely organized clandestine

---

SCHEDULE OF KING FERDINAND OF SPAIN AUGUST 2, 1492

9:00 A.M. Expel some Jews.

10:00 Expel some more Jews.

11:00 Expel all remaining Jews.

11:05 Expel a guy we missed.

12:00 Lunch, siesta.

3:00 P.M. Expel any Jews who have confessed since noon.

4:00 Bon voyage party for Columbus. Topic: If he should reach the Orient, would he please expel any Jews he finds there?

5:00 Meeting with the Portuguese. Topic: Ask them if they would mind expelling their Jews over to us so we can expel them again.

"O God, Thou hast appointed me to watch o'er the life and death of Thy creatures; here am I ready for my vocation. Now cough, please."

—*Maimonides' Extremely Reform "Prayer for Physicians"*

---

religious services, which they rarely bothered to attend.

By the end of the fifteenth century, Extremely Reform Jews had been expelled by virtually every country in Europe and by several planets in the Trifid Nebula.

Extremely Reform Jews accomplished a great deal during this period, despite harsh treatment. In philosophy, the great Jewish

EXTREMELY REFORM DIASPORA TRAVEL TIPS (HASSLE-FREE WAYS TO BE A MIGRANT PEOPLE)

Rule 1: Learn an easily transportable trade (e.g. moneylender, hairstylist, persecution consultant).

Rule 2: Sew name tags into all your *yarmulkes*.

Rule 3: Travel light. The following basic items may be all you need:
- Toothbrush
- Change of underwear
- Drip-dry prayer shawl
- Torah scroll (with Itty Bitty Book light)
- Toilet paper (if fleeing to Eastern Europe)

Rule 4: Save your receipts. You may qualify for the "International Social Pariah Tax Credit."

philosopher, scientist, and religious thinker Maimonides wrote his classic *Guide for the Perplexed*, a best-seller among Extremely Reform Jews, most of whom remained perplexed. Maimonides was also one of the world's first great physicians, and many of his Extremely Reform disciples went on to specialize in dermatology. In commerce, Jews traded in dyes, textiles, furs, and precious stones, traveling to India and beyond, while at home their families invented the phrase "He never calls, he never writes."

Expelled from most of Europe, some Extremely Reform Jews fled to Poland, where "Hasidism" arose. This was an emotional, revivalist movement that emphasized piety, mysticism, fervent dancing, and big furry hats. Needless to say, it was the Extremely Reform Hasids who contributed the furry-hat theme. Others

EXTREMELY REFORM JEWISH MYSTICISM

"If you assign a numerical value to each letter of the alphabet, and then add up all the letters of all the words in the entire Torah, you will end up with an unbelievably huge number."

—*The Extremely Reform Book of Kabbalah*

YIDDISH (AS IF HEBREW WEREN'T HARD ENOUGH)

Possibly as early as the eleventh century, European Jews began speaking Yiddish, a mixture of Hebrew, a few other languages, and an extensive assortment of throat-clearing noises. Because it originated in impoverished villages *(shtetls)*, Yiddish had some limitations; for example, it contained no word for "golf." It did, however, contain 273 different ways of complaining about lower back pain. By the nineteenth century, great works of literature were being written in Yiddish, including Shalom Aleichem's classic play *It's Hard to Be a Jew (Schver tsu Zayn a Yid)*, and two of his lesser-known works, *It's Even Harder to Be a Carp* and *How Would You Like to Be a Smoked Whitefish?* Yiddish also produced the Nobel Prize-winning author Isaac Bashevis Singer and the Nobel Prize-winning adjective, *"fahblonjet"* (meaning "hopelessly lost" or "confused," as in "Those Extremely Reform Jews are really *fahblonjet"*). Today, Yiddish lives on in Jewish culture as an important source of bewilderment and alienation for the Extremely Reform Jew.

fled to the Ottoman Empire, where, in an atmosphere of comparative freedom and religious toleration, they developed hundreds of ways to cook chickpeas. Some of the great Extremely Reform astronomers and navigators of Spain and Portugal took refuge in Holland, where they taught the Dutch how to fold and unfold maps without tearing them. Still others sailed to the New World, where, in 1965, Jewish L.A. Dodger Sandy Koufax pitched a perfect game against the Cubs.

As Europe became more enlightened and industrialized, countries began to invite the Jews back, at first just for the weekend, then for longer stays. By the eighteenth and nineteenth centuries, many Jews actually enjoyed civil rights in Europe, though they were appalled by the Dreyfus Affair, in which the French government colluded in framing an innocent Jewish artillery officer for spying. How could it be, they wondered aloud, that a Jewish person could think of *artillery* as a *career?*

There was further persecution from Hitler's Brownshirts, Mussolini's Blackshirts, and pretty much anyone who had a shirt. These experiences, culminating in the Holocaust, made Jews realize that they needed a permanent haven from anti-Semitism. To the Extremely Reform Jew, Englewood, New Jersey, seemed a logical choice. Palestine was another option, though the school system there was not quite as good. Despite diplomatic efforts, a Jewish homeland ultimately had to be established through the bravery of small militant groups: the Haganah, which waged a courageous underground war, and the Hadassah, which held women's luncheons on strategic territory. By 1948, Englewood was finally theirs. (Coincidentally, in that same year Jews also founded the State of Israel. Jews around the world now enjoy a universal "right of return" to Israel—automatic citizenship for any who return—except for Extremely Reform Jews, who are offered a free coffee mug if they just stay where they are.)

> ## TWENTIETH-CENTURY MILESTONES IN AMERICAN EXTREMELY REFORM JUDAISM
>
> **1907** First Extremely Reform Jew in Hollywood changes name for show-biz reasons.
>
> **1915** First Extremely Reform Jew in New York joins the Mafia.
>
> **1928** First Extremely Reform Jew attends the Indianapolis 500.
>
> **1943** First Extremely Reform Jew orders a kayak from L.L. Bean.
>
> **1974** First Extremely Reform Jew in a trailer park tells *The National Enquirer* that he was abducted by aliens.

Today, Extremely Reform Jews are thriving throughout the United States and other countries. They have formed stable communities, worked hard at their jobs, raised wholesome families, and, in their spare time, completely taken over the banks and the newspapers.

2.

EXTREMELY REFORM BELIEFS AND VALUES
(A Fairly Short Chapter)

At a time of falling test scores and lax personal morality, it is not uncommon to hear the complaint, "This decline of Western civilization—isn't it all the fault of the Extremely Reform Jews?" This sort of negative thinking stems from the fact that whenever discussions of values and responsibility come up, Extremely Reform Jews can be heard muttering things like, "Oh no, not another lecture about safe sex." By and large, though, Extremely Reform Judaism is not the cause of changing values, but instead more a symptom of them. Like many Extremely Reform Jews, you may be thinking, "I want to help with this problem. I want to be involved. How can I become a symptom?" You can begin by improving your grasp of the core beliefs of Extremely Reform Judaism.

God Looks Like Casper the Friendly Ghost and Lives Up in the Sky. One of the first questions Extremely Reform Jews ask is "Do I really have to believe in God?" Yes, and for good reason. Without God, your donations might not be tax deductible. Also, the Talmud tells us that every Jew must be able to answer those who claim that God does not exist. This invariably leads to intense arguments between the true believers and the doubters, which end when the true believers start shrieking, "Stone them!"

Extremely Reform Judaism has proved the existence of God through a rigorous theological inquiry known as "The Four Incontrovertible Extremely Reform Proofs of the Existence of God":

Proof Number 1:   There Are Too Many Coincidences That Science Cannot Explain. Example: A cabdriver gives you the exact same advice your psychiatrist gave you—*even though the two have never met!*

Proof Number 2:   How Is It That the Israelis Manage to Grow All Those Oranges?

Proof Number 3:   Many Dumb People You Have Met Are Very Successful. (This implies intervention by an infinitely powerful, transcendent being, albeit with a quaint sense of humor.)

Proof Number 4:   Stonehenge.

Reason and logic, of course, can only take you so far. After that, you must consult the Time-Life Books on Mysteries of the Unknown.

The Chosen People. According to the Torah, the Jews have been "chosen" by God. This is a great burden for the Extremely Reform Jew, who must confront the whole panoply of issues raised by being Chosen, most notably, "What exactly am I Chosen for?" and, "Is there some sort of Annual Fee involved?" Many Extremely Reform Jews look beyond the obvious prestige of being Chosen and ask, "Credential-wise, wouldn't it be more practical to have a graduate degree?" Extensive fieldwork indicates that being Chosen will not get you a job or help you beat a speeding ticket, but that it can get you excused from jury duty if you make a big scene about it.

CHOSEN FOR WHAT?	
Traditional Jews	**Extremely Reform Jews**
Chosen by God to be "a light unto nations."	Chosen by God to be "a lite unto nations" (same sense of purpose and mission, but only half the calories).

The Messiah and Which Borough He Lives In. The Messiah will be a descendant of King David, whose arrival will usher in a new age of peace and moral perfection: The dead will be resurrected, the Ten Lost Tribes of Israel will reappear, all the stored frozen embryos will be born, airline deregulation will turn out to be a gigantic success, and there will be a universal "Healing of the Hemorrhoids." In addition, Jewish parents will stop pressuring their kids to be successful and a rookie forward out of Yeshiva will lead the NBA in scoring.

> "They shall beat their swords into ploughshares,
> And their spears into pruning hooks,
> And nation shall not lift up sword against nation,
> But instead shall clobber one another with ploughshares and pruning hooks."
>
> —*The Extremely Reform Prophecy of Isaiah*

Some Hasidic Jews believe the Messiah has already arrived, in the form of a charismatic rabbi from the Crown Heights section of Brooklyn. Extremely Reform Jews, however, consider it more likely that the Messiah would arrive in a safer neighborhood, such as Forest Hills or perhaps Riverdale.

Extremely Reform Ethics. Extremely Reform Jews face ethical questions all the time. For example: At what point in a relationship do you tell your lover that you had a nose job? While you are dating? When you are engaged? Or when your first child starts to look like Pinocchio?

In times of crisis, the Extremely Reform Jew may consult the Bible, particularly when desperate for something to read in a hotel room. Hotel room Bible study can lead even the Extremely Reform Jew to ask challenging questions, such as "How come the Gideon people never leave anything by Kahlil Gibran?"

The Bible is filled with ethical commandments, some of them "negative" (things you should not do), others "positive" (things you should do). Examples:

Negative: Thou shalt not wear gold lamé to services on the Day of Atonement.

Positive: Thou shalt positively not wear gold lamé to services on the Day of Atonement.

A few useful and practical Extremely Reform interpretations of biblical principles are listed below. Extremely Reform Alert: Please note that the second half of your hotel room Bible is *not* applicable to your religion.

ASSORTED ETHICAL PRINCIPLES

Traditional Jews	Extremely Reform Jews
Only justice shalt thou pursue, that thou mayest live.	If you don't go to law school, you will starve.
Love the stranger.	Tell the stranger you just want to be friends.
Do not gossip.	Do not gossip?
Harbor no grudge against thy neighbor.	Play racquetball with thy neighbor to alleviate free-floating hostility.
Act on the moral principles you profess.	Try not to profess too many moral principles.
No sex with sheep.	No sex with sheep.

Charity or *Tzedakah* (Professional Fund-raising Begins at Home). Though not religiously observant, Extremely Reform Jews are active in many philanthropic activities and services, ranging from the Extremely Reform Home for the Jewishly Ignorant to the American Federation of Jewish Nuns. Volunteer counselors also handle thousands of desperate phone calls every day at the 24-hour 1-800-AM-I-A-JEW? Emergency Hotline. (Most of the callers turn out to be Extremely Reform Jews.) Extremely Reform charities also organize interesting social and cultural events for people uncertain of their Jewishness, such as trips and cruises to the Holy Land or, actually, any holy land.

> "He who gives a coin to the poor is rewarded with six blessings, but he who makes a pledge to charity receives a free tote bag."
>
> —*The Extremely Reform Talmud*

EXTREMELY REFORM CHARITABLE ORGANIZATIONS

- **The Extremely Reform Boy Scouts of America**

  (No camping required)

- **The Extremely Reform Anti-Defamation League**

  (Protecting the Jewish community from very mild ethnic slurs)

- **The United Extremely Reform College Fund**

  (Because a vague religious identity is a terrible thing to waste)

The Law of Conservation of Jewish Behavior. This Extremely Reform principle, adapted from Newtonian physics, provides that "for each and every Jewish act, there is an equal and opposite non-Jewish act." Thus, if you do a small kindness for someone less fortunate than you, you are permitted to eat a shrimp cocktail. If you visit a sick person in the hospital, you may spend the Sabbath at a restricted country club. If you go out of your way to become a rabbi, you may marry a Seventh-Day Adventist.

3.
MAINTAINING THE EXTREMELY REFORM JEWISH HOUSEHOLD

One of the greatest challenges facing the Extremely Reform Jew is how to maintain a Jewish home and, if possible, a Jewish second home, preferably near the beach. You can make your home more Jewish by following a few of the simple Extremely Reform steps discussed in this chapter. In the end, your efforts will have been worth it, because your home will communicate a clear message to anyone who visits: "*Shalom. You are in the home of Jewish people who have no idea what the hell they are doing.*"

GETTING STARTED

1. Use spiteful Extremely Reform Yiddish curses around the house. (Example: "May one thousand *hasidim* marry into your family! May your *zaftig* new girlfriend turn out to be a man! May all of your income be taxable!")

2. Arrange your lawn statues to depict scenes from *Fiddler on the Roof.*

3. Plant a burning bush.

The *Mezuzah*: Should You Install One Even If You Have No Idea What It Is?

By all means. There is really no better way to affirm the Extremely Reform Jewishness of your home than to own religious artifacts that you find puzzling. The Extremely Reform Jew need only know that the *mezuzah*, the traditional "guardian of the home," is a small hollow case containing a tiny scroll of parchment, not unlike a fortune cookie except that a) *mezuzahs* are not edible and b) fortune cookies are not nailed to your house. Although it is said that a *mezuzah* protects your home from evil spirits, to scare off burglars, you will want to purchase a large non-religious dog.

Inside the typical *mezuzah* is a special parchment scroll of verses which the Bible commands us to inscribe on our doorposts and which say, in essence, "This *mezuzah* inspected by No. 32." Every doorpost in your house should have a *mezuzah*, and every time you pass by one, you should touch the *mezuzah* gently with your fingertips and then kiss your fingertips, until everyone in the household has the same flu symptoms. You should also say:

May God protect my going out and my coming in from now and evermore,

though it is common to abbreviate this to:

God, I'm late. Where is my umbrella?

Your *mezuzah* should be checked twice every seven years to make sure the tiny scroll is still legible, or once every 10,000 miles if you live in a winnebago.

> **"Among the beasts of the field, ye shall not eat of them that are shown mating on the Discovery Channel."**
>
> —*The Extremely Reform Book of Leviticus*

Observing the Jewish Dietary Laws (From a Distance). Another way to make your home more Extremely Reform is to wonder about, but not necessarily follow, the Jewish Dietary Laws. These are not to be confused with the Jewish Laws of Dieting, although both involve widespread rationalizing and

DIETARY LAWS

Traditional Jews	Extremely Reform Jews
Codify which foods may be eaten.	Codify which foods may be eaten with Sweet 'n' Low.

cheating. The Dietary Laws require you to eat food that is "kosher," i.e. "fit," "proper," or "inspected by fussy rabbis."

PROHIBITED SEAFOOD

Traditional Jews	Extremely Reform Jews
Will not eat shellfish.	Rarely order "Surf 'n' Turf."

Making foods kosher involves removing unwanted impurities, such as flavor. Blood, for example, is not kosher, so for a steak or roast beef to be kosher, it must be soaked, salted, washed, and drained until even trained bloodhounds are baffled by its scent. This process is described in greater detail in the Jewish bestseller, *When Bad Things Happen to Good Cuts of Meat*. Though the process is complicated, it is nothing compared to koshering a good diet soda.

The Extremely Reform Law of Inverse Pork Recognizability.

While the Traditional Jew completely shuns pork, the Extremely Reform Jew heeds the following rule: "The less a piece of pork actually looks like a pig, the less you need to worry about eating it." Hence a B.L.T. or Mu Shu Pork may be eaten with few qualms, whereas a whole roast boar with an apple in its mouth should be

PROHIBITED MEAT

Traditional Jews	Extremely Reform Jews
Will not eat meat from a cow butchered in an ordinary slaughterhouse.	Will not eat meat from a cow that died in its sleep, committed suicide, or perished in a tragic boating accident.

---

eaten only if necessary to advance one's career. Also, though there is little biblical treatment of the subject, it is not uncommon for Extremely Reform Jews to have concerns about sushi.

How to Kill a Kosher Farm Animal. Even if an animal is generally O.K. to eat, it is still not kosher if it has not been slaughtered according to a specific, religiously prescribed method of killing, followed for centuries, that is supposed to be merciful and sanitary:

HOW TO KILL A KOSHER FARM ANIMAL

Traditional Procedure	Extremely Reform Procedure
1. Farm animal must be killed by ritual slaughterer using a sharply honed knife that must not have a single nick on its blade.	1. Farm animal must be told that it has the right to an attorney.
2. Slaughterer kills animal with swiftness and certainty, cutting nerves and arteries with single stroke of knife.	2. Slaughterer kills animal with swiftness and certainty by making it view Barbra Streisand in *Yentl*.
3. Slaughterer inspects dead animal's internal organs for any signs of disease.	3. Slaughterer inspects dead animal's internal organs for any signs of foul play.

SEPARATION OF MEAT AND DAIRY

Traditional Jews	Extremely Reform Jews
Will not combine meat with milk.	Will not combine meat with chocolate milk.
Have one set of dishes exclusively for meat, another for dairy foods.	Have one set of dishes exclusively for cheeseburgers.

The Hat/Meat/Milk Distinction. It should not go unmentioned that, though you may not *eat* animals that are not kosher, you may *wear* pretty much any animal as soon as it becomes a hat. Also, because Jewish law clearly forbids you to combine meat with milk, you must wait hours after eating meat before you may drink milk, although, strangely, you may go swimming approximately forty-five minutes after lunch without getting a stomachache. These are just a couple of the many paradoxes in the rich tapestry of Jewish law.

A Note on Jewish China and Flatware Requirements. The observant Jewish family must own at least two sets of china and flatware for daily use, one solely for meat and the other solely for dairy foods, plus an additional two sets for daily use only during the Passover week. They should also own four sets of formal china and flatware for use on special occasions—two for most of the year and two for the Passover week—and, of course, serving pieces for all of these sets.

> "And God said unto Moses: 'You shall instruct thy people, "Do not mix meat with milk. Do not place a non-recyclable product in a recycling receptacle. Pile your newspapers, magazines, and flattened cardboard boxes in a big bundle, tied with string. Never put an old car battery out with the garbage.' "
>
> —*The Extremely Reform Book of Leviticus*

A Further Note on Jewish China and Flatware Requirements. In the interest of full disclosure, it should be mentioned that the foregoing **Note on Jewish China and Flatware Requirements,** though more or less true, has been paid for by a generous grant from the United States Council for the Promotion of China and Flatware.

KOSHER FOODS

Traditional Hekhshers	**Extremely Reform Hekhshers**
Ⓤ ☒ Ⓚ ⱱ Ⓚ Ⓚ K	✡MS✡
(Approved by an Orthodox rabbinical organization)	(Approved by Martha Stewart)

How to Find Kosher Food. In most supermarkets, you should be able to find foods that you can eat by looking for a "hekhsher," or "seal of approval" signifying that the food has been certified by a major religious authority as kosher. If you cannot get kosher-certified items where you live, fly someplace and request the kosher airline meal. If you are afraid to fly, stay home and have all your food dry-cleaned.

Remembering the Sabbath. (Helpful Hint: It's every weekend.) One of the best ways to make a home more Jewish is to remember the Sabbath. We do this to commemorate how God created heaven and earth in six days and then spent the seventh day at home, in his pajamas, scratching himself. The Sabbath is an island in time, a period of restful contemplation, during which thirty-nine different kinds of

COMMON SABBATH COMPROMISES

Traditional Jews	Extremely Reform Jews
Hire "*Shabbas goy*" to perform religiously prohibited tasks.	Hire "*Orthodox Jew*" to perform religiously required tasks.

labor are specifically prohibited by the Talmud, among them No. 12 ("working in the import/export business") and No. 33 ("driving a get-away car"). According to tradition, it is a time when you may not travel and you may not create, destroy, or even alter the shape of an object. These prohibitions were adopted in ancient times to address the age-old problem of people traveling around, creating and destroying things by altering their shape.

Preparing for a Sabbath. It is traditionally said that you should "welcome the Sabbath as you would a bride." Others say that you should welcome the Sabbath as you would a queen, which would seem to require an entirely different guest list (fewer relatives, more dignitaries). Determining the correct Sabbath analogy is beyond the scope of this book and is addressed in greater detail in the author's forthcoming work, *Sabbath Bride or Sabbath Queen? Another Pointless Jewish Argument*. For now, the following steps should help you get your own Sabbath under way.

Step 1. Spend the Week Planning a Big Friday-Night Meal. Traditionally, a Jewish family, no matter how poor, would scrimp and save the entire week so that the Sabbath meal could be a great feast. Then one of the family degenerates would blow the whole wad in a card game and there would be no money left for food. This in turn led to the development of fishballs.

Step 2. During the Week, Encourage Young Children to Work on a Jewish Craft or Project to Present on the Sabbath. Note: In general, Nintendo is not considered a "Jewish craft."

MAKE YOUR OWN *YARMULKE:*
AN EXTREMELY REFORM JEWISH CRAFT PROJECT

Step 1.   Find an old Mickey Mouse hat.

Step 2.   Tear off the ears.

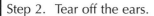

Step 3. At Sundown on Friday, the Mistress of the House Should Light the Candles. If you do not have a mistress, get one. Otherwise, have your wife do it. Do not sing "Happy Birthday" when the candles are lit. This is important Sabbath advice and goes for Hanukkah as well.

Step 4. Bless the Family. First, the parents bless the children:

May God keep you and bless you and you should win the Westinghouse Science Prize and become National Merit Scholars.

Then the husband praises his spouse with the traditional prayer "The Woman of Valor," a hymn to wifely virtue:

The woman of valor, seek her out,
For her price is far above rubies,
Not like those hookers who hang out near my office on Ninth Avenue.

The wife then nods in thanks and recites her own prayer, "The Man of Squalor":

Stop objectifying me with your patronizing,
male-supremacist religion.

Husband and wife then join hands and beseech God for a free *au pair*.

Step 5. Recite the Sabbath Kiddush. This blessing, based on the Book of Genesis and recited over a cup of wine, is included to remind us of the significance of the Sabbath observance:

And in six days the whole universe—sky, earth, and all their array—was completed, and so on the seventh day the Lord rested, and the Lord blessed the seventh day and called it holy, and then on the eighth day the Lord created a multitude of fake fossil records just to fool Charles Darwin.

Step 6. Serve Two Loaves of Challah. The second loaf of this special soft bread is needed to symbolize the double portion of manna the ancient Israelites received in the desert and also to serve as a "backup" or "standby" challah in case the first challah malfunctions. If you forgot to buy or bake two challahs, you must go all the way back to Step 1 and start over.

Step 7. Keep the Tone of the Dinner-Table Conversation Focused on Elevated and Holy Themes. Try to steer the Sabbath meal away from gossipy drivel (e.g. celebrity sex lives, the high jinks of the British royal family). Focus on important issues (e.g. Orthodox Jews Who Kill).

Step 8. **Oneg Shabbat** *or "Sabbath Delight."* Gather friends and family together and tell your favorite Bible stories. A popular old standby is the story of how Daniel survived being thrown into a den of hungry lions simply by praying. Daniel, of course, was a trained prophet, and you should not try this at home.

Step 9. Sing Jewish Songs **(Zmirot)** *That Convey the Joy of* **Shabbat.** Even the simplest Sabbath song can be filled with cheer. Many have been around for hundreds of years, and their enthusiastic renditions by ordinary peasant folk have been responsible for starting a number of pogroms.

TRADITIONAL SABBATH SONG

Shabbat, shalom,
We're trapped at home.

Chorus: Dai-dai-dai-dai-dai-dai-dai

O queen, O bride,
We're stuck inside.

Chorus: Dai-dai-dai-dai-dai-dai-dai

Shabbat, shabbat,
We can't do squat.

Chorus: Dai-dai-dai-dai-dai-dai-dai

(Repeat 93 times, clapping deliriously.)

Step 10. Rejoice in the Limitations the Sabbath Places on Your Life. Observing the Sabbath does not necessarily signify an inflexible retreat from the world. It signifies only that you are not allowed to do anything. This is the true blessing of the Sabbath: spending time with loved ones, contemplating Nature, and praying, e.g. *"O God, Creator of the Universe, Ruler of All Things, please let the Sabbath end before the dry cleaners close."*

SABBATH ELECTRICAL RESTRICTIONS	
Traditional Jews	**Extremely Reform Jews**
Believe that ancient Sabbath laws, as applied today, prohibit turning on electrical appliances.	Believe that it was always understood that these prohibitions were never to apply to the making of blender drinks.

Step 11. Saying Goodbye to the Sabbath. The Sabbath ends on Saturday evening as soon as three stars are visible in the sky, except in the Los Angeles area, where you just have to look at your watch. This moment is commemorated by a special ceremony, *havdalah,* which involves lighting a braided candle, sniffing from a fragrant spice box, and filling a wine cup to overflowing. Why the wine cup is supposed to overflow is unclear, though it may signify the ruining of a perfectly good tablecloth. This ceremony is so profoundly moving and rich in symbolism that many Jews forget to observe it altogether.

TRADITIONAL CHANT BIDDING FAREWELL TO SHABBAT

Alee-yo-hu ha-na-vee
Let's go see what's on TV.

Alee-yo-hu, ha-tish-bee
Let's go see what's on TV.

Alee-yo-hu, Alee-yo-hu
Let's go see what's on TV.

(Repeat until you are completely alone.)

4.

SYNAGOGUE SURVIVAL TIPS

The Traditional Jew goes to pray in a synagogue three times a day—morning, afternoon, and evening—every day of the week, a pattern that raises two important questions: 1) Does anyone in this religion actually work for a living? and 2) What night is bingo night? Unfortunately, Judaism does not have a bingo night, but there are other reasons for an Extremely Reform Jew to go to a synagogue occasionally, not the least of which is that if you never attend, you dramatically decrease your chances of being elected Treasurer.

Survival Tip Number 1: Synagogues Do Not Look Like Synagogues. Look for a modern, concrete building with about seventeen sides. If it is not a house of worship, it could be a House of Pancakes, which is not an entirely bad thing.

> "And God said to Moses: 'Let thy people build me a sanctuary, that I might dwell amongst them. And make sure it has a lounge and a community center, that I might have a place to schmooze. Also, an indoor swimming pool might be nice.'"
>
> —*The Extremely Reform Book of Exodus*

Survival Tip Number 2: To Tell Which Denomination It Is, Check the Parking Lot.

Orthodox Jews	Conservative/ Reform Jews	Extremely Reform Jews
No cars on Sabbath (strict observance of prohibition on driving).	Some cars (not-so-strict observance of prohibition on driving).	Sabbath Drive-Through Prayer Window.

Survival Tip Number 3: Wear a Hat. Just as the Jews are the "People of the Book," so they are the "People of the Hat." Jewish men have been wearing sacred round skullcaps since ancient times, possibly to hide male pattern baldness. The *"Yarmulke*-Club-for-Men" has grown exponentially over the years and now even includes the Pope, who has a white one. ("I'm not just the Pontiff—I'm also a client.")

> **"Cover your head, so that the reverence of Heaven be upon you. And take off that lobster bib."**
> —*The Extremely Reform Talmud*

Note: A high-numbered sunblock is no substitute for a *yarmulke* and vice versa. You would be surprised at how many Extremely Reform Jews make this simple mistake.

YARMULKES AND TOUPEES: A COMPARATIVE ANALYSIS

Yarmulke	Toupee
Easily detectable.	Easily detectable.
Difficult to wear while swimming.	Difficult to wear while swimming.
Rarely worn by TV-news anchormen.	Commonly worn by TV-news anchormen.

THE EXPERIENCE OF PRAYER

Traditional Jews	Extremely Reform Jews
Try to concentrate on prayers, achieve sense of being in the presence of the divine.	Try to figure out when to stand up, when to sit down, and what page everyone is on.

Survival Tip Number 4: During Services, Look for Somebody Who Knows What He Is Doing and Copy Him. Many Extremely Reform synagogues have only one really knowledgeable worshipper who unwittingly leads the whole congregation. This is usually the same person who knows exactly when to start applauding at the end of a Schoenberg concert.

ACCESSORIZING FOR PRAYER: AN EXTREMELY REFORM GUIDE

In addition to a **Yarmulke**, you may also want to wear a **Prayer Shawl (Tallit)**, a long, fringed white silk scarf that is used not only for solemn prayer but also for tying unsuspecting older worshippers to their seats. The wearing of the *tallit* is specifically commanded in the Torah, in the part where God says unto Moses, "Speak unto the children of Israel and bid them to wear white silk scarves, that while they pray they might look chic." As with *yarmulkes,* prayer shawls are like bowling balls in that some people own their own, while others use those provided by the synagogue (prayer shawls and *yarmulkes,* not bowling balls). However, unlike prayer shawls and *yarmulkes,* bowling balls rarely bear the gold inscription "In honor of the bar mitzvah of Buzzy Weintraub."

For daily prayer, you may also want to own a set of **Phylacteries (Tefillin).** These are small leather boxes, filled with scriptural verses, which the devout Jew binds with leather straps on his hand and on his forehead in accordance with the Talmudic injunction, "You shall follow all the instructions in the Book of Deuteronomy as literally as possible, even if it makes you look like an idiot and costs you all your friends."

Finally, apart from ritual attire, Jewish men generally wear **Neckties** to services, unless they are members of the Israeli Knesset, in which case an **Open-necked Sport Shirt** is more common.

Survival Tip Number 5: Drinking and Davening Do Not Mix.

Bowing, swaying, kneeling, and trembling in awe of the Almighty are fine, but only in moderation. Excessive humility can lead to back problems. Also, avoid davening while intoxicated (DWI), a practice that can lead to serious injury. If you are already intoxicated, have someone daven for you.

Survival Tip Number 6: No, You Don't Have to Know Hebrew. (Showing Up for Services Is Sufficiently Amazing.)

A question commonly asked by Extremely Reform Jews is, "Must I pray in Hebrew?" No, and wipe that look of terror off your face. Fluency in Hebrew, of course, is vital to the proper understanding of Israeli truck-driver insults. On the other hand, a famous Hungarian rabbi used to conduct his prayer services entirely in Hungarian. This does not mean you have to learn either Hebrew or Hungarian. It simply means that you can pray in any language you can actually speak. For example: In Brooklyn, New York, you might say, *"Yo! God! Blessed art Thou."* In Zuma Beach, California, the proper expression would be, *"Most Excellent Dude, I would rather pray unto you than go surfing.* Not!"

> **BASIC EXTREMELY REFORM HEBREW**
>
> *"Shabbat Shalom!"*—"Good Sabbath!"
>
> *"Ha Goldfarberim kanu yachta."*—"The Goldfarbs bought a yacht."
>
> *"Hi hishmina me'az hashana she'avra."*—"She's gotten heavier since last year."
>
> *"Ani hoshez she'ani mikabel hatkasat podagra."*—"I think I'm having a gout attack."

Survival Tip Number 7: The Prayer Book Is Read Backward, Not Forward.

Unlike this book, Jewish prayer books begin at what is normally the back of a book, and the pages are turned, left to right, until the front is reached. If you try this technique with, say, *Moby Dick,* you will note that Captain Ahab finds the great white whale right away, thus eliminating the need for about 700 pages of dense reading.

AN EXTREMELY REFORM PRAYER SAMPLER

The best way to become comfortable with a prayer book is to use it regularly. Since this is a serious problem for the Extremely Reform Jew, a quick summary is provided below.

"Borchu"—the *"Call to Prayer."* Usually recited at the beginning of the service, in the case of the Extremely Reform Jew it may take the form of a phone call the night before, e.g. "Hello, this is Rabbi Koppelman. We haven't seen you lately."

"Shema Yisrael . . . "—*"Hear, O Israel, the Lord our God, the Lord is One."* These are the most important words a Jew can know, apart from *"Quick, where are my pills?"*

The *"Shemoneh Esrei"* or *"Amidah"*—the *"Eighteen Benedictions."* This prayer actually consists of nineteen benedictions, but who's counting? The prayer is divided into three sections: Praise of God (the "Flattering and Buttering-Up Benedictions"), Requests That God Respond to Our Needs (the "Groveling and Whining Benedictions"), and, finally, Thanksgiving (the "Unbelievably Obsequious Benedictions"). The *Shemoneh Esrei* is sometimes also called the Silent Devotion, because it is read silently by worshippers, in memory of the persecution of Jewish mimes.

"Amen."—Loose translation: *"Ditto," "Count me in,"* or *"Me too!"* This prayer is an indispensable time-saver.

The *"Kedushah"* (*"Kadosh, kadosh, kadosh . . . "*)—*"Holy, holy, holy is the Lord of Hosts."* This prayer was written by the famous scribe Ezra the Repetitious and is very popular among the hard-of-hearing.

"Hazak, Hazak, Venithhazak!"—*"Be strong, be strong, and let us gather new strength!"* This is a special exhortation, recited when a congregation completes reading one of the Five Books of Moses. The Extremely Reform Jew shouts this prayer upon completing one of the Five Books of Tom Clancy.

The *Kaddish.*—This short praise of God is recited by mourners after the death of a family member, e.g. *"Magnified and sanctified be His great Name, Who just caused my dearest and closest relative to be hit by a bus. Any other brilliant ideas, O Great One?"*

The *Aleinu.*—One of the most sublime of all Jewish prayers, the *Aleinu* is one of the concluding prayers of the service and is followed by an immense sigh of relief. Loose translation: *"Yes, I know the Lord is One, but I just can't take it anymore."*

Survival Tip Number 8: When Praying, Never Call God by His Real Name. (He Doesn't Like It.) "God" is just a nickname, along with "Adonai," "King of Kings," Lord of Hosts," and "Slats." God's real name is "Y-H-V-H," the "ineffable tetragrammaton," a term so sacred that you should never say it aloud, not even

PRAISED BE THY NICKNAME	
Traditional Jews	**Extremely Reform Jews**
Upon seeing letters "Y-H-V-H" will not attempt to pronounce them.	Upon seeing letters "Y-H-V-H" will say, "Pat, I'd like to buy a vowel."

if you know the secret handshake. This is not really a problem, since no one knows how to pronounce it anyway.

Survival Tip Number 9: If Ever Called to the Pulpit by the Rabbi to Help Lead the Ceremony, Fake an Epileptic Seizure. Being called up by the rabbi (an *aliyah*) is a great honor, but it can involve opening the ark, handling the Torah, not to mention actual chanting. If you should accidentally get corralled into going up to the pulpit, do not "high-five" the rabbi. Also, as a matter of courtesy, do not heckle other worshippers who are trying to do an *aliyah* (e.g. never shout, "Don't quit your day job.")

WOMEN IN THE SYNAGOGUE: A SYNOPSIS

Historically, Jewish women have not been required or even allowed to engage in the same rites of prayer as men. Jewish feminists have dedicated their lives to the fight for equal prayer for equal work. Extremely Reform feminists have generally regarded their exemption from services as an excuse to catch up on their mail.

Traditional Judaism	Extremely Reform Judaism
Women not counted in *minyan,* the ten-person quorum for prayer.	What's a *minyan?*
Women not taught Hebrew or Torah.	Women not taught Hebrew or Torah. (Note: Who is?)
Women required to sit in balcony of synagogue, apart from men.	Women and men sit together, davening suggestively.
Strong disapproval of women rabbis.	Strong disapproval of topless women rabbis.
Married women required to conceal or remove real hair.	Married women required to conceal or remove real hair color.
Every morning men pray, "Thank you, O God, for not making me a woman."	Every morning women pray, "Thank you, O God, for not making me the Other Woman."

5.

THE JEWISH HOLIDAYS:
Feasting, Fasting, and Begging for Forgiveness
(The Extremely Reform Way)

How to Determine What Jewish Year It Is	How to Determine What Jewish Dog Year It Is
Add 3760 to current year.	Add 3760 to current year, multiply by 7.

The Jewish Lunar Calendar (One Small Step for Man, One Giant Leap for the Jews). The Jewish year is divided into ten lunar months, give or take a couple of months. (It's adjustable!) Because the lunar year is eleven days shorter than the solar year, constant corrections are needed to get the summer months to happen at the same time every year, preferably when it is not snowing. Months may have either twenty-nine or thirty days, depending on what year it is, and seven "leap months" must be added during every nineteen-year period. This has led to the most important principle of Jewish lunar time-keeping: "Show your math." The current Jewish calendar was officially adopted in approximately A.D. 358, according to the Gregorian calendar, or the year 4118, according to the Jewish calendar, a discrepancy that should have been

JEWISH TIME-KEEPING	
Traditional Jews	**Extremely Reform Jews**
Organize time according to lunar calendar.	Organize time according to lunar filofax.

an immediate clue that this calendar could be trouble.

The Jewish calendar is filled with religious holidays, and blundering through a few of them is an important Extremely Reform activity. Strictly speaking, the only holidays that are considered mandatory for Extremely Reform Jews are as follows: Rosh Hashanah, Yom Kippur, Passover, and Christmas. A few other optional holidays are mentioned (opposite), for Extremely Reform Jews interested in Extra Credit.

As a general principle, Jewish holidays are divided between days on which you must starve and days on which you must overeat. Many Jews observe no fewer than sixteen fasts throughout the Jewish year, based on the time-honored principle that even if you are sure that you are ritually purified, you definitely aren't. Though there are many feasts and fasts, there are no holidays requiring light snacking. (You can invent your own, e.g. the Extremely Reform Festival of the Pretzel Sticks.) Note: Unlike Christians, who simply attend church on special days (e.g. Ash Wednesday), on Jewish holidays most Jews take the whole day off. This is because Jews, for historical and personal reasons, are more stressed out.

THE YO-YO DIET GUIDE TO THE JEWISH HOLIDAYS

Rosh Hashanah—Feast.

Tzom Gedalia—Fast.

Yom Kippur—More fasting.

Sukkot—Feast.

Hoshanah Rabbah—More feasting.

Shemini Atzeret—Keep feasting.

Simchat Torah—Yet another feast.

Month of Heshvan—No feasts or fasts for a whole month. Get a grip on yourself.

Hanukkah—Eat potato pancakes.

Tenth of Tevet—Do not eat potato pancakes.

Tu B'Shevat—Feast.

Fast of Esther—Fast.

Purim—Eat pastry.

Passover—Do not eat pastry.

Shavuot—Dairy feast (cheesecake, blintzes, etc.).

Seventeenth of Tammuz—Fast (definitely no cheesecake or blintzes).

Tishah B'Av—Very strict fast (don't even think about cheesecake or blintzes).

Month of Elul—End of cycle. Enroll in Center for Eating Disorders before High Holidays arrive again.

"And you shall celebrate the New Year in the Seventh Month of the Year, and you shall not find this confusing, and it shall be a day of rest, except that you shall repeatedly blow the ram's horn until you cause an animal stampede."

—*The Extremely Reform*
   Book of Leviticus

Rosh Hashanah. This holiday, the Jewish New Year, is actually observed on the first day of the *seventh* month of the Jewish year, a peculiarity that Talmudic scholars have traditionally explained away as "just a scheduling problem." Rosh Hashanah marks the beginning of a peni-

"Thou shalt not stand outside the synagogue on the High Holy Days scalping thy tickets to the services."

—*The Extremely Reform Ethics*
   of the Fathers

tential period during which we contemplate our sins and try to remember which ones were worth it. In our prayers, we remind ourselves of our weakness, confess our wrongdoing, and beseech God for mercy, e.g. the *Avinu Malkenu* ("Our Father, our King"):

AVINU MALKENU
(Extremely Reform Version)

Our Father, our King! I have the right to remain silent.

Our Father, our King! I have the right to an attorney.

Our Father, our King! If I cannot afford an attorney, one will be provided for me.

Our Father, our King! Anything I say can and will be used against me in a court of law.

Our Father, our King! I understand these rights and wish to make a phone call before I say another word.

We also plead to be "inscribed in the Book of Life," based on the belief that God keeps three books open—the Book of Life for the good, the Book of Death for the wicked, and a third book for the intermediate. Thus, we ask God for forgiveness, while God asks Himself why He can never manage to finish a book that He starts.

> **"Who is like unto Thee, O God, who in Thy mercy rememberest Thy creatures unto life? Certainly not I, who cannot even keep a houseplant alive."**
>
> **—*Extremely Reform Rosh Hashanah Benediction***

During Rosh Hashanah services, we read the account of the Binding of Isaac, the story of how Abraham, following a commandment from God, almost killed his only son, Isaac, until God said unto him, *"And if*

HAPPY NEW YEAR!

Traditional Jews	**Extremely Reform Jews**
Spend eve of Jewish New Year at services, praying for mercy.	Spend eve of Jewish New Year in Times Square, waiting for ball to drop.

I told you to jump off the Empire State Building, would you do that too?" In the course of all of this, a ram's horn (*shofar*) is blown approximately 100 times, to wake sinners from complacency and also to wake anyone else. Rosh Hashanah is followed by ten days of penitence, perhaps for making so much noise.

Yom Kippur (The Day of Atonement). On this holiday, we castigate and punish ourselves, abstaining from all pleasures and comforts: We do not eat, bathe, anoint ourselves with oil (What? No anointing?), or even wear leather shoes. (In ancient times, leather shoes were considered a sign of great luxury, particularly if they were wing tips.) We recite many repentant prayers, including the ingenious *Kol Nidrei*, in which we get to atone in advance for all the promises we expect to break in the coming year. We also recite the Thirteen Attributes of God's

PERSONAL SACRIFICES ON YOM KIPPUR	
Traditional Jews	**Extremely Reform Jews**
Refrain from bathing.	Refrain from using loofah sponge.

AL CHEYT
(Extremely Reform Version)

For the sin which we have committed before Thee of buying a German car;

For the sin which we have committed before Thee of knowing the lyrics to a number of Christmas carols;

For the sin which we have committed before Thee of buying our winter wardrobe by mail from L.L. Bean, Lands' End, Eddie Bauer, J. Crew, and Talbots;

For the sin which we have committed before Thee of watching golf on television;

For all of these sins, O God of forgiveness, forgive us, pardon us, grant us remission.

> "O God, with respect to all vows and oaths, all promises and obligations, and pretty much anything we commit ourselves to from this Yom Kippur to the next . . . WE'RE JUST KIDDING!"
>
> —*The Extremely Reform Kol Nidrei*

Loving-Kindness (e.g. Attribute No. 9: "*He doesn't eat much.*").

One of the most important prayers of Yom Kippur is the *Al Cheyt* ("For the sin . . . "), a fairly specific list of our misdeeds, which we recite while beating our breasts in contrition.

The Yom Kippur services include the telling of the story of Jonah and the Whale, the ultimate narrative of redemption. This is a good time to reflect on what the story of Jonah and the Whale means for our times. Is it merely a lesson in God's mercy, or is it not, in fact, a cautionary tale about the dangers of bulimia? The point should be made that, with counseling, the Whale could have been helped.

Sukkot. Every autumn the leaves change color; pumpkins, squash, and wild corn ripen for picking; and a group of people gather for a festival meal, thanking God for His mercy in helping their ancestors survive in the wilderness. This meal, featuring stuffed turkey, cranberries, a parade, and several football games, is known as Thanksgiving and has absolutely nothing to do with this section of the book. This section is about the *other* festival meal

O MERCIFUL GOD	
Traditional Jews	**Extremely Reform Jews**
Thank God for giving Jews shelter in wilderness.	Thank Squanto for helping the pilgrims.

at which people thank God for His mercy in helping a bunch of ancestors survive in the wilderness, the Jewish holiday of Sukkot. On this holiday, instead of watching football, we are commanded by the Torah to "dwell in booths" to recall the meager shelter of the ancient Israelites:

> *Ye shall dwell in booths seven days that your descendants may know that ye dwelt in booths so that they may also dwell in booths, that their children might know about it too, and so on and so on. You know, a tradition.*

A "booth" (*sukkah*) is actually a leafy hut and must be fragile and open to the elements, symbolizing not just the plight of the Israelites but also centuries of Jewish building-code violations.

Apart from building huts, the most important symbol of Sukkot is the "four species" of plants—the willow, the palm, the myrtle, and the citron—bundles of which are ritualistically waved around and shaken each day of the week-long holiday, except on the last day, Hoshanah Rabbah, when the willows are beaten against the floor. Each day's prayers begin with a plea to God to save us, e.g. *"Save us, O God, for here we are, grown-ups, standing around, thrashing bundles of plants."* Sukkot prayers also incorporate deeply elegiac readings from the Book of Ecclesiastes, e.g. "Vanity of vanities, all is vanity! One generation passeth away and another cometh, yet the earth abideth and getteth into thy sneakers forever." (This is about as deeply elegiac as Extremely Reform worshippers get.)

Sukkot is immediately followed by **Shemini Atzeret,** one of the so-called Incomprehensible Holidays, and then by **Simchat Torah** (the Joy of Torah), the annual ceremony in which a congregation does a jubilant circle dance after reading the concluding passage of the Five Books of Moses (*"and then Moses sort of rolled his eyes and just keeled over"*).

Hanukkah. Hanukkah, the Festival of Lights, commemorates an event in Jewish tradition that is firmly rooted in documented historical fact. This aspect of the holiday is so refreshing and unusual that it alone is worth celebrating. Hanukkah commemorates the successful revolt of Judah the Maccabee against pagans who had oppressed the Jews and defiled their Temple. After their victory, the Maccabees had only enough holy oil to burn for one day, yet it burned for

> "And the Maccabees took back the Temple and made search and found a single cruse of extra virgin olive oil, sealed and pure, sufficient for but one day's lighting. And there was much weeping and wailing and gnashing of teeth, for there was no more oil, nor were there any extra virgins. But they lit the lamp with the oil and a miracle was wrought therein, for it burned eight days and nights, and the Maccabees gave thanks unto God, saying, 'Thank you, we had a wonderful cruse.'"
>
> —*The Extremely Reform Talmud*

THE CHRISTMAS TREE QUANDARY

Orthodox/ Conservative Jews	Reform Jews	Extremely Reform Jews
Absolutely no tree. Feel alienated from Yuletide festivities.	Buy small so-called "Hanukkah bush." Feel guilty, ambivalent.	Buy huge tree from old-growth forest complete with endangered spotted owl nest. Feel pretty good about the whole thing.

eight, hence the very moving Hanukkah prayer, *"Hear, O Israel, your mileage may vary."*

We commemorate this miracle by lighting a menorah, a nine-branched candelabrum: one candle for each day of Hanukkah, plus the ninth *shammes*, or helper candle, that is used to light the others. (To conceptualize this in an Extremely Reform way, think of each of the eight candles as a reindeer—Dasher, Dancer, Prancer, Vixen, Comet, Cupid, Donner, and Blitzen—with Rudolph as the *shammes*.) We also sing songs, eat potato pancakes *(latkes)*, give gifts, and play a game of chance and wagering using a special spinning top *(dreidel)*, a toy invented by the great medieval Rabbi Menachem the Compulsive Gambler of Lemberg. To save time, many Extremely Reform Jews celebrate all eight days of Hanukkah on one day, December 25, using a pine tree instead of a menorah. (Helpful Hint for the Kids: Leave some *latkes* and a glass of milk for Santa.)

Purim. This holiday commemorates how the evil Haman tried to kill Mordechai the Jew and all the other Jews of Persia, only to be executed himself, thanks to Queen Esther, the King of Persia's Jewish wife. In contrast to Hanukkah, this account apparently has no factual, historical basis, and perhaps for this reason, on Purim we really whoop it up. We hold elaborate costume parties, make a tremendous racket using noise-makers *(graggers)*, and, to comply with an actual Talmudic dictum, are supposed to get so drunk that we "cannot tell the difference between the blessed Mordechai and the cursed Haman." (This is not all that drunk when you consider that the Talmud also says, "You know, to me, all those ancient Persians look alike.")

Perhaps the high point of every Purim, though, is the Purim play, in which parents proudly watch their children play-act the Purim legend:

GLENGARRY GLEN PURIM
(A Purim Play in One Act)

by

David Mamet
(for ages 6–12)

HAMAN: F——. You should kill that f——ing Mordechai and all those f——ing Jews.

AHASUERUS, KING OF PERSIA (*wearing slippers with upturned toes to show he is Persian*): F——. Queen Esther says I should f——ing kill you instead.

HAMAN: F——ing kill me? (*pause*) That's just f——ing great. You're going to f——ing listen to her?

AHASUERUS: F——. (*pause*) She baked me a f——ing three-cornered pastry.

HAMAN: A f——ing three-cornered pastry?

AHASUERUS: A f——ing *three-cornered* pastry.

HAMAN: So. (*pause*) You're going to f——ing kill *me* instead of Mordechai because she baked you a f——ing *three-cornered* pastry?

AHASUERUS: I think it's called a "*hamentaschen*." (*pause*)

HAMAN: F——.

Passover. Passover, like Easter and professional baseball contract disputes, is a rite of spring. It began long ago when God freed the Jews from bondage in Egypt by visiting the homes of the Egyptians and killing their first-born. To make sure that God skipped Jewish homes, the Jews killed a lamb and marked their lintels with its blood. (At that time, it was common to mark things with the fresh blood of a lamb if nobody nearby happened to have a pen.) The markings worked and God "skipped" them.

Markings Used by Israelites to Ward off Death

JEWISH FIRST-BORN ON BOARD

Ever since then, every year, we celebrate the "skipping" with a great feast. "Skip," however, was deemed unacceptable as a name for a religious holiday, as were "Skipper" and "Skippy," all of which were denounced by ancient sages as "a bunch of dumb nicknames generally applied to household pets and college roommates." Instead, after long deliberations, the ancient sages labeled the festival "pass over" or simply "Passover," because it had never been used as a nickname by anyone. The name "Dead Lamb" was not seriously considered at all. Because Passover is such an unbelievably complicated holiday, an entire chapter is devoted to it (at no additional cost to you, the reader). (See page 45.)

Shavuot. In ancient times, Shavuot was a great harvest celebration, in which, after a great procession to the Temple, the Israelites delivered an offering of the First Fruits of their harvest. The Jewish High Priest would then touch and squeeze every single fruit to see if it was ripe, furtively eating a grape or two. Shavuot is also the day on which God revealed His law to the Jews at Mount Sinai. There is vehement debate among Jewish denominations over whether God revealed just part of His law at this time, e.g. the Ten Commandments, or whether He revealed the entire Torah. To Extremely Reform Jews, it seems pointless to continue to squabble, especially now that both have been disclosed for years and are even widely available in paperback.

> **"Thy God shall be my God and thy people shall be my people. And thy people on the coast shall be my people on the coast. And thy people shall call my people and we'll do lunch. *Ciao!*"**
>
> —*The Extremely Reform Book of Ruth*

Despite its importance as a holiday, Shavuot has few formal rites, though there are some, such as the reading of the Book of Ruth. (Extremely Reform Alert: The Book of Ruth is part of the Bible and has nothing to do with baseball.) We also light memorial candles for King David, a descendant of Ruth, who is said to have died on Shavuot, and we read his psalms (e.g. Psalm 23, "*. . . Surely goodness and mercy will follow me all the days of my life and I will dwell in the House of my parents forever.*") Finally, on Shavuot, Jews celebrate by eating dairy products, following the ancient sage who is said to have exclaimed, "What kind of a religion is this that nobody has to eat cheesecake?"

Tishah B'Av. This is the saddest, darkest day of the Jewish calendar, the day on which a number of really terrible things happened to the Jews. On this day, the First Temple was completely demolished by the Babylonians; then, roughly six centuries to the day later, the Second Temple and the city of Jerusalem were completely demolished; and then, on the same day almost two thousand years later, Woody Allen's reputation was completely demolished. This is a day of fasting, lamentations, and dirges, including a special dirge for Marv Levy, the only Jewish coach in the National Football League, who led the Buffalo Bills to an unbelievable, record-setting, four successive Super Bowl losses. Extremely Reform Jews observe this day by adamantly refusing to get out of bed.

A Final Note on the Jewish Holidays. This Extremely Reform summary omits a number of holidays, such as Yom Hashoah (Holocaust Remembrance Day), which is too depressing, and Tu B'Shevat, which has something to do with trees. If you really want to know about these and other holidays, you will have to wait for the author's multivolume work-in-progress, *The Jew Who Knew Too Much: A Guide to Religious Holidays That Nobody Can Spell or Pronounce.*

6.

THE EXTREMELY REFORM PASSOVER HAGGADAH
(or "Why Is What Night Different From All Other Nights?")

A Main Selection of the Haggadah-of-the-Month Club!

What Is a Haggadah? A Haggadah is the book used to guide everyone through the Passover meal or "Seder." The Prague Haggadah of 1526 was the first to be printed and illustrated. The Extremely Reform Passover Haggadah is the first to offer a "scratch & sniff" bitter herbs feature.

The Searching for Leaven. Before Passover begins, we must rid our homes of every last crumb of leavened bread. The Extremely Reform Jew will instantly recognize this search as a sort of Easter Egg hunt, except that we don't decorate the bread crumbs with watercolors. Be-

---

> **SCRATCH & SNIFF HERE**
>
> (Think about the smell of horseradish. Think really hard. This won't work if you don't make an effort.)

---

cause bread crumbs, unlike Easter Eggs, are difficult to distinguish from carpet lint, this job should not be left until the last minute. Indeed, to make life easier, we deliberately place pieces of bread in several rooms. We also say a prayer to thank God for commanding us to search for the bread, even though we know exactly where the bread is, since we hid it ourselves:

Thank you, O God, for commanding us to find the Bread that we just hid.

We do not stress to God how incredibly *easy* it is to find bread that we hid ourselves. We want God to think this is a big deal so we can hit Him up for favors in the future.

Setting the Passover Table. On the table there should be three pieces of *"Matzah"* (Unleavened Bread), which may be in any shape, round or square, though usually not in the shape of a nativity scene. Passover matzah is called *sh'murah* matzah, because it is "guarded" or "watched" by rabbis to make sure that it does not become contaminated or leavened during the baking process. On some occasions, the rabbis stop guarding the matzah and instead eat it with Extra Crunchy Peanut Butter. This is called *"a midnight snack."* In ancient times, the three separate matzahs symbolized the three separate classes of Jews—Cohens, Levites, and Israelites. Today, the three matzahs symbolize doctors, lawyers, and furriers.

There should also be a Passover Plate, which can be made of virtually anything—wood, metal, stone, or porcelain. (A paper Passover Plate is generally not used, unless you are planning a Passover Picnic.) This plate holds, among other things, the Roasted Lamb

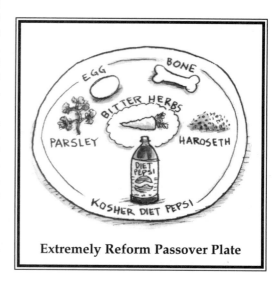

Extremely Reform Passover Plate

BAGELS AND MATZAH: A COMPARISON

Bagels	Matzah
No dotted lines.	Dotted lines.
Not flat.	Very flat.
Hole in middle.	No hole in middle.
Available in pumpernickel.	Not available in pumpernickel.

Shankbone and a Hard-boiled Egg. There is great debate over whether these ritual items should actually be eaten at the Seder. Some scholars believe that the Lamb Shankbone and Egg are supposed to be purely symbolic. A contrary school of thought, led by several housewives in Coney Island, maintains, "There are people starving in Africa! If you don't eat everything, it will just have to be thrown out, which is a crime."

The plate also holds a green vegetable, such as parsley, and a bitter herb, such as horseradish or romaine lettuce. These items, which no one really wants to eat, are in fact reluctantly swallowed by everyone later in the Seder. One other item on the plate is a mixture called *haroseth*, made of chopped apples, cinnamon, ground nuts, raisins or dates, and a little wine. The Extremely Reform Jew will instantly recognize this as a Waldorf salad without the mayonnaise.

You will also need a saucer of salt water or vinegar. The significance of this and all the other Passover foods is explained later in the Seder. Why later? Because part of being an Extremely Reform Jew is not really knowing what is

THE EGG

A symbol of fertility and regeneration, the Egg is common to Passover, Easter, and other spring holidays. In ancient times, the Greeks, Persians, and Chinese all exchanged eggs at their respective festivals. The precise reason for egg-swapping is not known, though it may have been simply an understandable urge to get the best possible egg. Some rabbis say that the Passover Egg represents life itself: Both are oval, smooth, and slightly off-white in color. These rabbis are now in therapy.

THE LAMB SHANK

To protect themselves and propitiate the gods, many ancient societies sacrificed a lamb or a goat or, if they were vegetarians, a zucchini or a melon in the shape of a lamb or goat. Some ancient cultures even practiced human sacrifice. Translations of early stone carvings include phrases like: "You know, it tastes just like chicken!"

---

going on. This is nothing to be alarmed about.

Finally, don't forget to provide an extra goblet for the Prophet Elijah, who visits every home on Seder night. Additional goblets may be placed at the table for any other invisible friends you may have invited, but don't overdo it: This is a Seder, not a seance.

What to Wear. The leader of the Passover Seder wears a *kittel*, a white robe with lace down the front and at the cuffs. This robe is also worn by the Jewish male at his wedding and at his funeral, usually in that order. The fact that it is a burial shroud is a reminder of our short time on earth. Wearing a burial shroud on joyous occasions is just one of those things that we Jews, as a people, get a kick out of.

How to Sit. At Passover, we place a pillow on each chair so we can recline comfortably while eating. This practice dates back to Roman times, when such luxury was the mark of a "free man," or, in modern terms, a "couch potato." By telling us to celebrate Passover with bad posture, the Talmud is squarely in conflict with proper parenting, not to mention Emily Post. Regrettably, the Talmud does not explain how to eat while reclining, e.g. how to drink without dribbling; should you eat food that lands on your stomach?; what do you do when your arm falls asleep? Note: Do not leave a chocolate mint on each pillow; we are celebrating Passover, not room service.

Reciting the Kiddush. We begin the Seder with the Kiddush, a blessing recited over wine. We thank God for choosing us, exalting us, giving us festivals and holidays and seasons for rejoicing and joy and happiness. This is definitely an upbeat prayer and not the right time for whining and complaining. The Kiddush includes additional prayers of thanks when the Seder falls on the Sabbath. Thus, if the Seder is held on a Friday evening, the Extremely Reform Jew should add to his prayers: *"Is it Friday already?"* If it falls on a

RAISE YOUR CUP	
Traditional Jews	**Extremely Reform Jews**
Thank God for the Fruit of the Vine.	Thank God for Fruit of the Loom™.

Saturday evening, he should add the following: *"Is it Saturday already? Where did Friday go?"*

HOW PASSOVER WINE IS MADE

1. Grapes are grown and picked under the supervision of rabbis. Each grape is individually inspected, checked for color, and rabbinically fondled.
2. The grapes are ritually stomped in accordance with Jewish law (i.e. by people wearing galoshes).
3. The grape juice is collected in barrels, where it is combined with chicken soup for better fermentation.
4. The wine is sniffed by the Head Rabbi. The Head Rabbi inhales the vapor of the wine into the upper part of his nasal cavity where long, thin nerves convey the sensation to special Jewish cells in the right side of his brain. These remarkable brain cells help the Head Rabbi evaluate the bouquet: Is there anything "foreign" or "wrong" with it? Is there any hint that the bouquet is, perhaps, "too gentile"? These are just some of the questions that the Head Rabbi must ponder before proceeding to a certification.
5. The Head Rabbi tastes the wine, swirling it in his mouth and across his palate, and considers the final question: "Are we really supposed to drink this stuff?"

Drinking the First Cup of Wine. In the course of the Passover festival, we drink four cups of wine. Some Jews, especially in Israel, drink a fifth cup to commemorate the return to the promised land. Many are now in twelve-step programs, trying to cut back. ("My name is Yonkel. And I'm an alcoholic.")

Before drinking, we say the following prayer:

> *Blessed art Thou, Eternal our God, Ruler of the universe,*
> *Creator of the fruit of the vine.*

We do not ask God whether Manischewitz really comes from a vine, but it is certainly fair to wonder. Note: Pregnant women who drink the four cups of wine are risking Fetal Manischewitz Syndrome (babies are born with a bad taste in their mouths).

The Washing of the Hands. This ritual cleansing was done at the Temple in ancient times. By washing our hands now, we express hope that the Temple will be rebuilt speedily and that redemption will come in our lifetime. By scrubbing thoroughly, we express hope that all the younger members of the family will some day become surgeons.

Eating a Green Vegetable *(Karpas)*. Passover is a rite of spring, a celebration of the liberation of Nature. In ancient times, pagans welcomed spring by holding a drunken, frenzied Bacchanalian orgy. The Jewish tradition, by contrast, has been to eat roughage with one's relatives. *Karpas* means, literally, "grass or vegetation," but the Extremely Reform Jew should stick to eating edible plants. (Religiously speaking, you get no additional points for devouring a hanging fern.) We usually nibble a piece of parsley dipped in salt water. The green of the parsley symbolizes rebirth, renewal, and the verdant fields of spring. The salt water symbolizes the tears the Israelites shed in Egypt. Nibbling reminds us of the cruelty of Pharaoh, who sadistically required all the Israelite slaves to nibble.

DOUBLE DIPPING	
Traditional Jews	**Extremely Reform Jews**
Dip parsley in salt water.	Dip Belgian endive in balsamic vinegar.

Breaking the Middle Matzah and Hiding the *Afikoman*. Here, the middle matzah is broken into two pieces, one of which is hidden somewhere in the house (see page 58). The remaining piece of matzah stays at the table as a symbol of affliction (the "bread of affliction"). Many of our relatives and in-laws stay at the table for the same reason (the "relatives and in-laws of affliction"). Then we lift the matzah and recite a traditional summons to prayer:

All who are hungry, let them come and eat; all who are needy, let them come and celebrate the Passover with us. Now we are here, next year may we be in the Land of Israel. Now we are slaves, next year may we be free men. And perhaps the year after that, we will take a nice vacation someplace. But who can plan that far in advance?

Lifting the plate is an invitation to all, a call to the street, to the ghetto, to the *shtetl,* and, indeed, to the whole world to hear the story of Passover. In short, it is a conference call. Though we invite the hungry and needy to join us, it is not essential that they actually show up, so long as at least one of our financially successful guests leads a life that is empty and meaningless.

The Four (Extremely Reform) Questions. Passover requires each parent to be a teacher, each child a student, each dining room a study hall. This does not mean we have to redecorate. It does mean, though, that before telling the story of Passover, we ask the youngest person present at the Seder to ask The Four Questions. For some reason, most Jews keep asking the same Four Questions, year after year. The Extremely Reform Jew will make a more wide-ranging inquiry, such as:

   I. Who invented gefilte fish and why?
  II. If Rabbi Akiba has five bitter herbs and Rabbi Gamaliel asks to borrow three bitter herbs, how many bitter herbs will Rabbi Akiba have left? (Students of the Dead Sea Scrolls will recognize this as a trick question.)
 III. Shouldn't coffee rings be kosher for Passover?
  IV. When do we eat?

Because the purpose of the Seder is, in part, to educate, it is considered praiseworthy to ask additional questions throughout the Seder. For example, at any time during the Seder one may ask, "But is it good for the Jews?" Still, it is not praiseworthy to ask questions incessantly. If someone does this, it is considered praiseworthy to ask him to shut up.

The Five Sages Pull an All-Nighter. It is written that the five great sages—Rabbi Eliezer, Rabbi Yehoshua, Rabbi Elazar ben Azaryah, Rabbi Akiba, and Rabbi Tarfon—once stayed up all night discussing the Passover Seder until their pupils came to them and said, "Our masters, it is time to recite the morning *Shema*." Rabbi Elazar ben Azaryah said, "Here am I a man of seventy years and never could I prove that I had been served regular coffee when I asked for decaf, until Ben Zoma expounded it thus: 'Though it is said that "the orange-handled carafe is for decaf," still a waiter may fill it with regular coffee.'" The other sages then expounded it thus: "It had to have been regular coffee, or why would a bunch of seventy-year-olds be up all night like this?"

This story shows that even the wisest person can keep learning from Passover, and furthermore, that the five sages were completely *meshuggah*.

Blessed be the All-Present, blessed be He, and so on and so forth.

The Four Sons (Who Are So Different from Each Other They Must Have Been Adopted). The Extremely Reform Jew must learn to tell the story of Passover in different ways for different listeners. The Torah tells you to imagine that you have four sons—one who is wise, one who is wicked, one who is simple, and one who does not know how to even ask a question. To the wise son, you must explain the story of Passover down to the tiniest detail. To the wicked son, you must say, "Why can't you be more like your brother Chaim, the smart one?" To the simple son, you must explain, "Pay no attention to the wicked son, who is a bum and will never amount to anything with his terrible attitude." To the son who is unable to ask questions, you must say, "Speak up! What am I supposed to be, a mind reader?" No matter how you decide to explain Passover, you are not supposed to change the basic plot, i.e. the Jews get enslaved but then escape.

The Extremely Reform Story of Exodus. Here the leader of the

Seder and the guests take turns reading aloud the biblical account of the miraculous rescue:

In the beginning our ancestors prayed to many gods. As it is written: "In days of old, our forefathers lived beyond the river and worshipped idols. And to walk humbly with thy god involved lugging around a heavy statue. Now we worship the Eternal, because of His covenant with our father Abraham. For the Holy One said unto Abraham: 'You will worship Me and only Me. In exchange, thy children will be strangers in a land not their own. They will be enslaved there and be afflicted for four hundred years. And by the way, you are all going to have to be circumcised. Any questions?'"

Raise the cup of wine.

And this covenant has sustained us, for more than once they have risen up against us and tried to destroy us, in every generation they try to destroy us, but the Holy One, blessed be He, always delivers us, though not right away, as it is written: "Please allow six to eight weeks for delivery."

Put down the cup.

A wandering Aramean was my father. It made for a difficult childhood. But enough about my problems. For it came to pass that Jacob and his sons went down to Egypt, as it is written: "And Jacob said to Pharaoh, 'To sojourn in the land we have come, for there is no pasture for our flocks, since the famine is sore upon the face of Canaan.'" And Pharaoh said, "I had sores like that once. You should spend less time in the sun."

And the children of Israel were fruitful and increased abundantly and waxed mighty, as it is written: "And the children of Israel mightily increased the abundance of waxed fruit."

And the Egyptians did evil unto us, as it is written: "And

Pharaoh said unto his taskmasters, 'The children of Israel are waxing too much fruit. Let us do evil unto them.'"

And we cried unto the Eternal, the God of our fathers, and the Eternal heard our voice, and He saw our affliction, and our toil, and our oppression. And He said unto us, "If thou thinkest this is bad, wait till thou seeest what happens to Job."

But God remembered His covenant with Abraham, with Isaac, and with Jacob, and He said unto His people: "A covenant is a covenant. I will rescue you and bring you to the land of milk and honey, which is not as sticky as it sounds."

And the Eternal brought us forth from Egypt, not by the hand of an angel, not by the hand of a seraph, not by the hand of a messenger, not by the hand of Alan Dershowitz, but by Himself, in His glory and in His Self, as it is written: "And I will pass through the land of Egypt on that night, and I will smite all the first-born in the land of Egypt, both man and beast, and against all the gods of Egypt I will execute judgment. It is I the Eternal and not an angel, I and not a seraph, I and not a messenger, I and not Alan Dershowitz."

And the children of Israel girded up their loins and wrapped sackcloth around them, for no particular reason. And then the children of Israel took coconuts and almonds and chocolates and egg whites before they had leavened and bound them up in their clothing. And they made macaroons of the coconuts and almonds and chocolates and egg whites which they had brought forth from Egypt, as it is written: "Bake for twenty minutes or until brown; let stand; serve when cool." For they were thrust out of Egypt and could not tarry, neither had they prepared for themselves any toll house cookies.

EXODUS TIMELINE

Birth of Moses. Infant Moses is hidden in bulrushes, found and raised by royal family.

Birth of Shirley MacLaine (in a previous life).

Moses slays a cruel Egyptian slavemaster. Flees country after being profiled on *Egypt's Most Wanted*.

Working as shepherd in desert, Moses sees burning bush and interprets divine message: Breed flame-retardant sheep.

God tells Moses, "You cannot see My face, for man cannot see Me and live." Moses gathers that God looks like a blind date he once had.

Hoping to free the Jews, Moses tries to frighten Pharaoh by performing magic and miracles with shepherd's staff. Pharaoh is unmoved.

Moses calls a shepherds' staff meeting. Moses' Vice President for Signs and Wonders and his Administrative Assistant for Plague Implementation make strong presentations.

Plagues ensue. In case death of Egyptian first-born doesn't persuade Pharaoh, Moses has backup plan: spontaneous combustion of second-born.

Pharaoh is convinced. Tells Israelites to depart by 11 A.M., so rooms can be readied for afternoon slave arrivals.

Pharaoh changes mind and chases Israelites to Red Sea. Ignores metro traffic report: "Red Sea is closing in, with both lanes coming to a complete halt and massive drowning likely."

Egyptian chariots become tangled in beach towels and volleyball nets and are unable to escape total destruction.

The Spilling of the Drops of Wine. Here, we dip our fingers into our wineglasses and spill drops of wine to show our compassion for the suffering caused by the plagues God inflicted upon the Egyptians, even though they were our mortal adversaries. "For if a man shows no mercy," said the ancients, "what difference is there between him and a beast?" (Note: For one

Traditional Plagues Visited on Egyptians	Extremely Reform Plagues Visited on Egyptians
Blood, Frogs, Vermin, Wild Beasts, Cattle Disease, Boils, Hail, Locusts, Darkness, Slaying of the First-born.	Low Self-Esteem, Difficulty Performing in Bed, Early Morning Panic Attacks, Acute Pyramido-phobia (intense fear of pyramids).

thing, a beast can't play the harmonica.) The Jews are a caring people and do not gloat over victory. Indeed, if we happen to run into an Egyptian at this time of year, we do not say things like, "Pharaoh sucks!" or, "Too bad, sarcophagus breath!" Instead, we speak words of consolation, such as, "Have a nice day!" (One final note: The more drops of Passover wine you spill in memory of the plagues, the less you actually have to drink.)

Singing "Dayeinu." This is the first of several unbelievably repetitive Passover songs that the Extremely Reform Jew will find exhausting to sing (particularly the one about the goat and two *zuzim*). *"Dayeinu"* commemorates a long list of miraculous things God did for us, any one of which would have been pretty amazing just by itself. *"Dayeinu,"* translated literally, means, *"Thank you, O God, for overdoing it."*

Explaining the Passover Offering. At every Seder we recall the statement of Rabbi Gamaliel, who said: "Whoever has not explained the meaning of the Passover Offering, the Matzah, and the Bitter Herbs at the Seder on Passover has not fulfilled his duty." Because of this observation, many scholars consider Rabbi Gamaliel, of all the great rabbis, to be the biggest nag. Actually, at this point in the Seder even the Extremely Reform Jew will have picked up much of the symbolism and will get the rest later. Those who do not should attend the second Seder, traditionally held on the second night of Passover (the "Remedial Seder").

DAYEINU
(Extremely Reform Version)
(with apologies to Cole Porter)

He brought us out of Egypt,
executed judgment against our enemies,
did justice to their idols and slew their first-born.
It's delightful, it's delectable, it's Dayeinu.

He gave us their property,
divided the sea for us,
brought us through it on dry land and drowned our oppressors.
It's delightful, it's delectable, it's Dayeinu.

You can tell at a glance
that on this night, Pharaoh had no chance,
you can hear Mother Nature murmuring low—
"Let my people go!"

He helped us for forty years in the desert,
gave us manna and the Sabbath,
and brought us to Mount Sinai.
It's delightful, it's delectable, it's Dayeinu.

He gave us the Torah,
and brought us into the Land of Israel,
and built for us the Holy Temple where we could atone for our sins.
It's delightful, it's delicious, it's delectable, it's delirious, it's dilemma,
  it's delimit, it's deluxe, it's Dayeinu!

Drinking the Second Cup of Wine. Why do we drink a second cup of wine? Because switching drinks would result in a much more serious hangover. Thus, we stick with wine.

Washing the Hands (Again). A large bowl of water is brought to the table and we wash our hands as before, saying the following prayer:

Blessed art Thou, Eternal our God, but didn't we just do this
a few minutes ago? Who created this ceremony, Lady Macbeth?

Blessing and Eating the Matzah, the Bitter Herbs, and the "Hillel Sandwich."

Here, one says a blessing for bread *(motzi)* and unleavened bread *(matzah)*. If anyone named *Mitzi* is present, bless her too. Then eat a small piece of matzah. After that, bless the bitter herbs, dip them in the *haroseth,* and eat them. Jewish lore has it that, in ancient times, Rabbi Hillel "put matzah and bitter herbs together and ate them as a sandwich." This is the so-called "Hillel Sandwich," which you should also eat. Other Extremely Reform Passover Sandwiches include:

No. 7—The Akiba (lamb shank and roasted egg with cole slaw on pumpernickel)

No. 12—The Eliezer (parsley, salt water, and Russian dressing on light rye)

No. 94—The Moses (gefilte fish and boiled carrot on loaf of manna)

(All of the above served with sour pickle.)

The Festival Meal. The meal may begin with a number of traditional appetizers, e.g. hard-boiled eggs, matzah ball soup, and gefilte fish. The eggs are dipped in salt water, symbolizing the Red Sea, while the eggs themselves help you visualize your relatives in bathing suits. Matzah balls are a traditional food, invented by Spanish Jews in the fifteenth century, and many of the original matzah balls of that period are still in use today, possibly in your home. Finally, the gefilte fish is a mysterious creature whose habitat and mating habits have never been well understood, though most of them are believed to come from jars.

After these dishes, the traditional Jewish household often serves a steaming potted brisket. Extremely Reform households, on the other hand, may opt for a free-range chicken on the theory that if our ancestors wandered in the wilderness for forty years, so should the main course.

Dessert consists of cakes and cookies that are kosher for Passover (i.e. baked without yeast or leavening) and, because of this religiously inspired method of preparation, have an otherworldly taste and texture (i.e. baked on the planet Neptune).

The Afikoman. After the meal, the children play a game in which they try to find the small piece of matzah previously hidden by one of the adults (see page 51). The child who finds it must then ransom it back to the leader of the Seder in exchange for a prize, such as a silver dollar. This simple game actually teaches children a useful lesson: that grown-ups will pay good money for hidden crackers. Once ransomed from the clutches

> ## THE GREAT *AFIKOMAN* SEARCH
>
> | Traditional Jewish Child | Extremely Reform Jewish Child |
> | --- | --- |
> | Looks for hidden piece of matzah. | Looks for Waldo. |

of the child, the crumbled piece of matzah is divided among everyone at the table and eaten. The word *afikoman* itself means "dessert" or "the last thing to be eaten," after several ancient sages said, "That's the last thing I want to eat."

Saying Grace with Henry Kissinger. It is customary for the leader of the Seder to lead the grace. When an important guest is present, however, it is customary for him to be given the honor of leading the grace:

(RESPONSIVE READING)

HENRY KISSINGER: *Let us say grace.*

ALL ASSEMBLED: *May the name of Henry Kissinger and of the Eternal be praised from now and for evermore.*

HENRY KISSINGER: *May my name and the name of the Eternal be praised from now and for evermore. With the permission of all present, let us praise Him of Whose food we have eaten and in Whose goodness we live.*

HOST OF THE SEDER: *Who invited Henry Kissinger?*

ALL ASSEMBLED: *Praised be He of Whose food we have eaten and in Whose goodness we live. Praised be He and praised be His name. Praised be Henry Kissinger and praised be his name too.*

HENRY KISSINGER: *Thank you.*

Drinking the Third Cup of Wine. Guests who refuse to drink another cup should be sternly informed that this is a serious religious obligation. If they still refuse, they should be sternly informed that this is an old college

THE FOUR GULPS	
Traditional Jews	**Extremely Reform Jews**
Drink four cups of Manischewitz.	Belt down four Manischewitz Jell-O shots.

drinking game and that losers must finish the Seder in their underwear.

Opening the Door for Elijah

Opening the Door for Elijah.

At some point in every Seder, we open the door for Elijah the Tishbite, a great prophet who, according to the Bible, never actually died but instead ascended to Heaven in a fiery chariot. He is said to visit the Jews frequently, showing up at Seders every year and helping the poor. Inevitably, he has been called "the Elvis of the Old Testament prophets," though others prefer to think of Elvis as "the Elijah of the rock-and-roll drug abusers." Many devout Jews believe he will one day resolve all disputes in Talmudic law (Elijah, that is, not Elvis).

Because of Elijah's reputation for aiding those in distress, there are many famous stories about him, handed down through the generations, such as these two:

It was the first night of Passover and Shmuel, a poor villager who made his living bundling sticks of wood together, had no money for his family to have a Seder meal. No one was buying his bundled sticks, and his only other product, bundles of mud, was not exactly a crowd-pleaser. But Elijah knew Shmuel to be a good and observant Jew who, through no fault of his own, had been dropped on his head as an infant. And so, mounting his chariot, Elijah sped down from the heavens and drove to the man's house. "Behold, I am the Prophet Elijah! Who among you is Shmuel, Maker of Worthless Bundles?" he announced to a surprised gathering.

Tentatively, one of them replied, "My name is Hersh. I am a cardiologist. Who is Shmuel?"

Sensing the possibility of a mistake, Elijah asked what year it was, only to be told, "1973."

"Damn!" he said. "I knew I made a wrong turn. I was aiming for around the Second Crusade."

Of course, Elijah ultimately found poor Shmuel and helped him somehow.

It had been a very long and hard winter, food had become quite scarce, and the villagers, poor but devout, went to their Rebbe to pray for help.

Elijah heard their prayers, mounted his chariot, and went to the village. With tears of gratitude, the Rebbe greeted him.

"As you can see," he said, "I am a simple servant of God and my people are humble peasants and laborers. Our needs are very modest."

"Your needs, their needs, everybody's needs," Elijah responded. "How come we never talk about *my* needs?"

And Elijah got back in his chariot and went into therapy.

The Skimming of the Really Long Prayers.

The final segment of the Seder is the reading of the Hallel, a prayer in praise of God that consists of some of the most sublime and lyrical of the Psalms of David. Unfortunately, after three full cups of wine and a heavy meal, who can be bothered? Skim the psalms and **Drink the Fourth Cup of Wine.** By now, kosher wine should actually taste pretty good.

> "Pour out Thy wrath upon the nations that know Thee not, pour out Thy rage upon them and let Thy fury overtake them, pursue them in anger and destroy them. And if You can manage it, O God, please do this in the nicest, most polite way possible."
>
> *—Extremely Reform Prayer Recited upon Opening Door for Elijah*

KEY CHARACTERISTICS OF PASSOVER SONGS

1. The album cover contains a warning label to minors, e.g. **CAUTION: Lyrics are highly redundant; English translation of Hebrew may not rhyme.**
2. The subject matter of the song harkens back to a simpler time, when buying a goat was a career move.
3. No one in your extended family can agree on a melody.

The Humming and Mumbling of the Traditional Songs.

The Seder ends with the singing. Jewish homes ring with the gay sounds of Seder guests humming and mumbling the traditional Passover songs. Some of these songs, such as *"Had Gadya,"* have so many verses and refrains that they can take hours to complete, which may be one reason Passover caroling has never quite caught on. Some scholars interpret these songs as important allegories of Jewish history, while others find them merely a nuisance.

Ended Is the Extremely Reform Passover Seder.

Next Year, at Someone Else's House!

7.

THE EXTREMELY REFORM CYCLE OF LIFE

The stages of Extremely Reform Jewish existence are generally demarcated by a few major "life-cycle" events—Birth, Bar or Bat Mitzvah, Intermarriage, and Death. (One new major phase: Downward Mobility.)

Circumcision. The circumcision, or *brit milah,* a covenant sealed in flesh, is the Jewish

---

THE UNBROKEN CHAIN

Traditional Jews	Extremely Reform Jews
Struggle to maintain religious standards of previous generation.	Struggle to maintain standard of living of previous generation.

---

way of affirming, "There is a God," or at least, "After this, there better be." We do it because God ordered Abraham and all his descendants to be circumcised, so it is mandatory, unless you can prove that you are not related. Every Jewish son should be circumcised shortly after birth. If you procrastinate, and your son has already left for college, expect an argument.

JEWISH LAWS OF DESCENT

Orthodox/ Conservative	Reform	Extremely Reform
Child is automatically Jewish only if mother is Jewish.	Child is automatically Jewish if either mother or father is Jewish.	Child is automatically Jewish if obstetrician is Jewish.

> **"Before beginning the procedure, always make sure the child is male."**
>
> —*The Extreme Reform* Mohel *Training Manual*

The circumcision is performed by a *mohel*, Hebrew for "medical school dropout." *Mohels* do thousands of these operations, and some have made The Guinness Book of Records in the category "Most Penises Handled." To date, no *mohel* memoir or biography has been made into a television miniseries.

The ceremony itself is quite brief. The infant is held in place by a *sandak* or "holder," often the infant's godfather, who uses a half nelson or scissors hold or, if necessary, simply sits on the child. It cannot be stressed often enough that, despite the seeming cruelty of operating without anesthesia, the infant feels absolutely no pain. And so, let us repeat it: *The infant feels absolutely no pain.*

PAINLESS CIRCUMCISION PROCEDURE

1. The *mohel* says a prayer:

   *Blessed are You, O God, who commanded us to cut off the tip of the penis of this child, who, of course, will feel **absolutely no pain.***

2. The foreskin is cut, **completely painlessly.**

3. An additional subincision is made to prevent the foreskin from growing back. This step in the procedure is **especially painless.**

4. Red wine is placed on the lips of the screaming infant, who pees on the *mohel.* This is the child's way of saying, "Thank you, and I am **not in any pain."**

5. Family and friends repair to a joyous meal.

6. Male guests who have witnessed the ceremony become sexually dysfunctional and require counseling.

Generally speaking, the circumcision is the last major procedure of this kind to be performed on a Jewish boy unless, later in life, he discovers that he is a woman trapped in the body of a man.

For female infants, there is no ceremony quite comparable to a circumcision, though when they are grown up they may be forced to read a copy of *Backlash*.

NAMED FOR GREATNESS	
Traditional Jews	**Extremely Reform Jews**
Name child after historic diplomatic breakthroughs, such as Balfour Declaration of 1917 (e.g. "Rabbi Balfour Brickner").	Name child after contemporary diplomacy, such as U.S. aid to Israel (e.g. "Loan Guarantee Schwartz").

Naming the Extremely Reform Child. According to superstition, the Almighty inscribes each person's particular fate in His record according to the name he or she has been given (although the Almighty supposedly had to use a different system during the "Jennifer" craze of the 1970s). Indeed, the Talmud tells us that the most important thing a person can have is a good name. In spite of all this, every year a shocking number of Jewish newborns continue to be named "Brittany." If you doubt the serious implications of choosing a name, simply go to a crowded area, call out, "Hey, Steve!" and watch what happens. Then go to another crowded area and yell, "Hey, Mephiboseth!" and notice the difference. Then go home and stop making a nuisance of yourself.

Jewish children are typically given Hebrew names in addition to their legal names. The Hebrew name is used in traditional rites (bar mitzvahs, marriage ceremonies, federal indictments) and usually has some special significance (see box).

A Hebrew name can also be combined with the patronymic *ben* ("son of"), thus identifying the father

Traditional Jews	**Extremely Reform Jews**
"Yehiel"—"may he live"	*"Marshall"*—"may he become a partner in a corporate law firm"
"Yoseph"—"may God grant us another"	

NAME CUSTOMS AND THEIR REASONS

Ashkenazic Jews	Sephardic Jews	Extremely Reform Jews
Custom:		
Naming a child after a dead relative.	Naming a child after a living relative.	Naming a child Cody or Cheyenne.
Reason:		
To honor the dead.	To honor the living.	To honor Wyoming.

of the bearer of the name: Rabbi Eleazar ben Judah (Eleazer, son of Judah), Rabbi Simeon ben Gamaliel (Simeon, son of Gamaliel), Rabbi Isaac ben Paternity Suit (Isaac, son of a guy who has been asked to submit a DNA sample).

Because of the importance of a name to a child's identity and self-image, it is not altogether uncommon for Extremely Reform parents to seek out names that resonate with symbolic significance. It is also not uncommon for Extremely Reform Jews to change these names later in life. For more on this whole subject, see Chapter 93: What to Do If Your Parents Named You After an Endangered Species.

> **"David comforted his wife Bat Sheva, and she bore him a son. He was called Billy Bob and the Lord loved him."**
>
> —*The Extremely Reform Book of II Samuel*

Raising the Extremely Reform Child.
Young people's lack of knowledge about their Jewish heritage is widely acknowledged to be the greatest threat to the

Traditional Jewish Mother	Extremely Reform Jewish Mother
Overprotects children.	Leaves children in overprotective day-care center.

survival of Judaism. Many rabbis complain that the typical Extremely Reform Jew can easily name five U.S. presidents, but not five Talmudic scholars. (Actually, this is not quite accurate. Most Extremely Reform Jews *cannot* easily name five U.S. presidents.)

The transmission of Jewish awareness to the Extremely Reform child is primarily the responsibility of the Extremely Reform parent. It is, after all, the Extremely Reform parent whom the inquisitive Extremely Reform child first confronts with the question, "What religion are we?" And it is the Extremely Reform parent who typically responds, "Why do you ask? Are you some sort of religious fanatic or something?"

EXTREMELY REFORM CHILDHOOD ROLE MODELS

- Marcel Proust (half Jewish)
- Benjamin Disraeli (born Jewish, converted to Christianity)
- Sigmund Freud (Jewish atheist)
- Franz Kafka (Jewish, yet demented)

EXTREMELY REFORM CHILDREN'S BOOKS

- *The Grinch Who Celebrated Christmas*
- *Babar Gets His Trunk Fixed*
- *Curious George Dates a* Shikse
- *Winnie the Pooh Eats Piglet*

WHY *DO* EXTREMELY REFORM CHILDREN GO TO CHRISTIAN PAROCHIAL SCHOOLS?

1. In contrast to Hebrew day schools, at Christian parochial schools all prayers are said in English, a major advantage.

2. Jewish children learn valuable lessons there, e.g. how to communicate effectively with nuns.

3. Studies show that Jewish kids in Christian schools acquire the same cognitive skills as other kids, while getting to take off twice as many religious-school holidays.

As time goes by, the Extremely Reform child will rely on the Extremely Reform parent for answers to many other difficult questions, such as, "O.K., so if I'm Jewish, how come I go to a Christian parochial school?"

Raised correctly, Extremely Reform children should be able to give the following tortuous response when asked about their religion: "My mother is Jewish by birth but not practicing and my father was christened as a Catholic but does not currently believe in God, so I am technically Jewish but do not have to have a bar mitzvah unless I want one and have been told I should reach my own decision which I expect to do by the time I am nine."

STAGES OF JEWISH EDUCATION

Traditional	Extremely Reform
Child must take Hebrew lessons whether he likes it or not.	Child must take ballroom dancing lessons whether he likes it or not.
After just a few years, can read Hebrew and Torah, and has had some exposure to Talmud and Mishnah.	After just a few years, can waltz and fox-trot, has had some exposure to lindy and Charleston.
Child attends Jewish summer camp, sings Jewish folk songs around campfire.	Child attends non-sectarian summer camp, sings folk songs about the principle of separation of church and state.
Child spends years in preparation for bar mitzvah.	Child spends six weeks preparing at Stanley Kaplan Extremely Reform Bar Mitzvah Review Class (simultaneously picking up pointers for college boards).
As teenager, is sent to Israel as part of student exchange program.	As teenager, is sent to Europe in exchange for the children of lapsed French Catholics.
Attends Yeshiva College while living at home.	Goes away to Ivy League university while parents turn room into a study.

EXTREMELY REFORM YESHIVA: COURSE OFFERINGS

Introduction to Extremely Reform Judaism—Students will be introduced to some of the elementary principles of being Jewish in a cultural sense, including, "No human sacrifice," "No running around the swimming pool," and "Never trust a surgeon who advertises on the subway." Students will also study the lives of famous Jews who changed their names (e.g. Beverly Sills, a/k/a "Bubbles" Silverman) and take at least one field trip to see actual observant Jews in their natural habitat. Term Paper: "Everything I Have Learned About Judaism" (100-word maximum).

Beyond Manischewitz: Extremely Reform Alcohol Consumption— Jews brought up in traditional households do not appreciate just how many ways there are to get really drunk. Taught by Chaim "Pool Bar" Shlivovitz, this course exposes students to the exciting world of Extremely Reform drinking at all socioeconomic levels—how to drink six beers without undoing the six-pack, how to order alcohol by its brand name (Tanqueray & Tonic, J & B on the rocks, Colt 45 in a brown paper bag), how to say, "I'll have a bourbon and branch," and mean it. Lab work: supervised Jewish martini mixing and tasting. (Hint: Try a prune instead of an olive.) This course, or its equivalent, is a prerequisite for Beyond Manischewitz II: Extremely Reform Alcoholics Anonymous.

Introduction to Israel-Bashing—Students will begin by learning to express mild disagreement with Israeli policies and gradually work toward foaming at the mouth from both a right wing and left wing perspective. Includes field trips to the United Nations and the State Department, visits from Pat Buchanan and Noam Chomsky. Term Paper: 3,000 words on the statement, "I am not a self-hating Jew; I just hate other Jews."

Really Long Jewish Films—This class will focus on Jewish film-making, with an emphasis on movies and documentaries that are three hours long or at least that seem that long. Films covered will include *The Sorrow and the Pity, Shoah, Hotel Terminus,* and anything featuring Robby Benson. Course topics will include technical aspects of film-making as well as tips on bladder control during screenings. Class project: making a World War II documentary longer than the War itself.

The Problem of Evil and Why Won't It Go Away—Why is there evil, and why won't it go away? Why do the righteous suffer and the wicked prosper? What are earthquakes for? How can the same team make the playoffs one year and stink the next? These questions will be repeated annoyingly throughout the semester. The class focuses on the Book of Job, examining how trials and tribulations can serve as a test and giving useful tips to students who don't test well. The class will also discuss why there is sex and violence in the Book of Genesis and whether there is enough. Course prerequisites: Grousing I and Grousing II (Advanced). Term Paper: 2,000 words on "Why Life Sucks."

The Extremely Reform Bar Mitzvah ("Today I Am a Man. Tomorrow, I Will Be a Seventh-Grader.") The bar or bat mitzvah, held on or near a child's thirteenth birthday, is the date when a Jewish child reaches adulthood and assumes full responsibility for his transgressions and personal discipline.

FEMALE RITES OF PASSAGE: SOME BASIC DISTINCTIONS

Bat Mitzvah Ceremony	Debutante Cotillion
Lots of Jews.	Very few Jews.
Very few debutantes.	Lots of debutantes.

Hereafter, when a Jewish teenager misbehaves, he himself is responsible for saying, *"O God, I have sinned against Thee. I am therefore grounded for a week."*

THE EVOLUTION OF THE MODERN BAR/BAT MITZVAH

- Ancient Africa: To prove manhood, youth must spear, cook, and eat a wild animal.
- Ancient Israel: To prove manhood, youth must spear, cook, and serve wild animal to guests at elaborate sit-down banquet.
- A.D.13:   Bar mitzvah of Jesus Christ—Young Jesus performs first miracle, turning a single piece of puff pastry into huge Viennese-dessert table. (Caterers are impressed.)
- 15th Century: To appease Inquisition, Spanish Jews replace *hava nagila* with conga line.
- 20th Century: A "theme" bar mitzvah gets completely out of hand when a wealthy Long Island family rents the Aircraft Carrier *Nimitz* and entertains guests with aerial bombardment of Lebanon.

EXTREMELY REFORM BAR/BAT MITZVAH PROCEDURE

1. The child is called up to recite the bar mitzvah blessing:

   O my God and God of my fathers, on this solemn and sacred day, which marketh my passage from boyhood to manhood, I humbly venture to raise my eyes unto Thee and to declare, with all sincerity and truth, that I simply do not recognize 90 percent of the relatives in this room. In my earliest infancy, O God, I was brought within Thy sacred covenant with Israel through the act of circumcision, which, combined with my lack of adequate early breast-feeding, has left me an embittered and alienated adolescent. Today, I again enter into Thy community and undertake henceforth to bear the responsibility for my actions toward Thee, at least in theory. In the event that I really screw up, I expect to be treated as a minor and let off with a warning. Try to remember, O God, that it's not like I asked to be born.

2. The child reads aloud a portion of the Torah, followed by a portion from the Prophets (the Haftorah), e.g.

   And the Prophet Ezekiel spake: "The word of the Lord came unto me saying, 'Behold, a son of man shall turn thirteen and receive fountain pens and savings bonds and several copies of Bartlett's Familiar Quotations, *though of course cash gifts will be gratefully accepted. And there shall be a great feast and much noshing, but his voice shall crack and he shall get really tenacious acne and it shall be upon his face and shall not pass, nor shall any ointment work, no matter what the commercials say.'"*

3. The father of the child blesses him and recites the traditional prayer thanking God for the fact that his son has reached maturity:

   Blessed be He who has released me from the responsibility for raising this boy. Yippee! Hooray! I'm a free man! As my final act as a father, O God, I promise that after this ceremony I will take my son aside and explain to him the concept of massive student loans.

4. The child delivers a speech on what the bar mitzvah means to him. This speech varies tremendously depending on the expectations of the community. Thus, in an Orthodox service, the child would have to deliver a learned disquisition on the Torah. In an Extremely Reform service, he is permitted to make a statement using hand puppets.

5. There is a catered reception, involving "just family and friends" (in the Houston Astrodome).

How to Deprogram Your Extremely Reform Teenager After He Has Joined a Religious Cult.

This sort of thing can be tremendously annoying. A few suggestions, if it happens to you:

Step 1: Reach out with unconditional love. Tell your child that you understand his need for a sense of belonging and his search for new experiences, even if his actions happen to be stupid and degrading and a social embarrassment to the whole family. Ask him if he's met any nice Jewish girls in the cult. Explain that you still love him and that you will always be there for him, even though

RELIGIOUS CULTS	
Traditional Jews	**Extremely Reform Jews**
Jews for Jesus.	Jews for Moses.

you have legally disinherited him. (It is best not to tell him about the detectives you have hired to kidnap and deprogram him.)

Step 2: Adapt to the situation. If you cannot persuade your child to leave the cult, encourage him to excel within it. Spur him on to become First Assistant to the Swami, Executive Vice President for Chanting and Mind Control, or, ideally, the cult's Doctor-on-Call.

Step 3: Be opportunistic. Book your child on *Donahue*.

NEW-AGE EXPERIENCES	
Traditional Jews	**Extremely Reform Jews**
Have out-of-body experience.	Have out-of-Judaism experience.

Extremely Reform Marriage. Marriage is such an important institution in Judaism that, in biblical Hebrew, there is no word for "bachelor." There isn't even a polite, biblical way to say, "How about if we just live together for a while and see how we feel." Indeed, not marrying is considered

COMMON PARENTAL FEARS	
Traditional Jews	**Extremely Reform Jews**
Fear that child might marry a non-Jew.	Fear that child might have a one-night stand with a Kennedy.

so serious that the Talmud teaches that those who do not marry are to be nagged and hounded and sent out on blind dates and have personal ads placed in their names without their knowledge by meddlesome relatives. Very religious Jews believe that marriages are predestined by God, a view that Extremely Reform Jews share, although Extremely Reform Jews also believe that God predestines most of these marriages to end badly.

Recent surveys show that as many as 50 percent of all Jewish marriages are to non-Jews. On the bright side, other surveys show that 50 percent of all marriages end in divorce. On the other hand, still other surveys show that many divorced Jews remarry non-Jews. At some point, it is believed, 100 percent of all Jews will have to answer some sort of survey.

> "And God said, 'It is not good that Adam should be alone. I will make a helpmeet for him.' And God took a rib from Adam while he slept. And God said unto Adam, 'Behold, I have made for you a WASP named Katherine.' And they were both naked, man and wife, and were not ashamed, for they had not either of them any parent threatening to disown them."
>
> —*The Extremely Reform Book of Genesis*

Intermarriage ("You're Not Losing a Jew, You're Gaining a Unitarian!"). Traditionally, Jewish families responded to intermarriage by officially declaring the offending child dead. With modern advances in medical technology, however, this approach has

> "Let me not to the marriage of true minds
> Admit impediments; however, in your case
> Let me point out a few problem areas."
> —William Shakespeare,
> *Extremely Reform Sonnet No. 116 ("To an Interfaith Couple")*

simply become less and less believable. Today, intermarriage is a two-part process: first, gently breaking the news to one's family, and second, finding a way to stay on speaking, shouting, or at least glowering terms.

Stage 1: Extremely Reform Parental Notification.

> *EXAMPLE A:* "Mom and Dad, I am going to marry Bart. Yes, I know, he's a blue-eyed Aryan monster, but he's not like other blue-eyed Aryan monsters."

> *EXAMPLE B:* "Mom and Dad, I am going to marry Jorbel. Yes, I know, she's a Baal-worshipper, but she's not like other Baal-worshippers."

Stage 2: "Togetherness Activities" for the Interfaith Family.

Religion	Activity
Jewish/Catholic	Feeling guilty together.
Jewish/Hindu	Refusing to eat either pork *or* beef.
Jewish/Islamic Fundamentalist	Listening to Cat Stevens albums together.

WHEN A JEW MARRIES A JEW:
THE PROBLEM OF INTRA-MARRIAGE

The most alarming thing about marriage statistics is that they show that as many as *half* of all Jewish marriages involve *one Jewish person* actually marrying *another Jewish person.* This is a trend that threatens the very future of Extremely Reform Judaism. Among the dilemmas facing the intra-faith couple: what sort of explanation to give to friends and relatives ("You're not going to believe this, but . . . "), what sort of wedding ceremony to have ("Do we have to have . . . a *"rabbi?"*), and, most challenging, how to raise the kids. (Many children of intra-faith marriages become confused when told, "Mommy is Jewish, but Daddy is also Jewish.") Below, candid confessions of recently married intra-faith couples:

Jews Who Married Jews

"My mother kept saying 'Where did we go wrong?' but after a while she simply accepted him for what he was, her son-in-law, who happened to be Jewish."

"Deep down, I wished she weren't Jewish. It would have felt more 'right.' Finally, I decided, 'I guess I can handle this.'"

"I had heard of Jews marrying Jews and was aware it could happen, but I was sure I wouldn't let it happen to me. He just slipped in under my radar. I guess my defenses were down."

"We discussed it over and over and finally decided that maybe it would be easier if one of us converted to something else. I offered to be the one, but she insisted it be her, and then I felt guilty and converted too. Now we're both Scottish Presbyterians and our families are very upset. It's a complicated situation."

The Extremely Reform Wedding.

Step 1: The Marriage Proposal. This is the first formal step toward marriage, though it is actually preceded by three informal steps, "The Living Together for Several Years," "The Ticking of the Biological Clock," and "The Issuing of the Ultimatum."

Step 2: Selecting a Date for the Wedding. This is a bad idea. Never bring a date to your wedding.

Step 3: The Boycotting of the Wedding by Relatives Who Disapprove of the Bride, the Groom, or Something. This important step requires no effort and generally happens automatically.

Step 4: The Veiling. Ever since Jacob was tricked into marrying Leah instead of Rachel in the Bible, it has been customary for grooms to see the bride just before the ceremony to make sure there have been no late substitutions or snafus. At an Extremely Reform Wedding the bride must provide two

---

THE PURCHASING OF THE ENGAGEMENT RING

Traditional Jews	Extremely Reform Jews
Groom haggles fiercely in 47th Street diamond district, gets real bargain.	Groom pays way too much at Cartier, gets superb gift-wrapping.

BACHELOR RITES: THE "AUFRUF" VS. THE BACHELOR PARTY

"Aufruf"	Bachelor Party
Ancient ritual ceremony held in synagogue.	Neanderthal ritual ceremony held in topless bar.
Groom recites portion of Torah.	Groom's friends recite off-color limericks.
Groom is pelted with nuts and candy.	Groom is pelted with panties.
Groom is center of attention.	Topless dancers are center of attention.

---

types of I.D. and her dental records. The bride's face is then covered with a veil and the rabbi blesses her, quoting from the Book of Genesis:

RABBI: *O Sister! May you grow to be the mother of thousands of myriads.*
BRIDE: *Thanks a lot.*

Step 5: The *Huppah*. The bride and the groom proceed to the *huppah*, a canopy made of four poles and cloth. The *huppah* symbolizes the marital home and is actually a fairly accurate replica of the kind of home the young newlyweds will be able to afford. The parents of both the bride and the groom stand at the edge of the *huppah* to remind the bride and groom that just because they are getting married doesn't mean they should expect any privacy.

Step 6: The Bride and Groom Drink from the Same Cup of Wine. As they perform this rite, the bride and groom gaze adoringly at each other, as if to say, "You didn't spit in this, did you?"

Step 7: The Recital of the Vows and the Ring Ceremony.

RABBI: *Do you take this woman to be your first wife?*
GROOM: *Uh, sure.*
RABBI: *Do you take this man to be your first husband?*
BRIDE: *Mmm . . . what?*
RABBI: *I now pronounce you first husband and wife.*

The groom then puts the ring on the bride's finger, reciting: *"Behold, you are consecrated unto me with this ring, in accordance with the law of Moses and Robert Moses and Grandma Moses."* The wedding ring should be simple and unadorned, though not so simple and unadorned that it starts to rust in a few days. The bride then recites, *"I am my beloved's and my beloved is mine, and my is beloved am and beloved mine I is, and am I . . ."* until the rabbi silences her.

Should the bride give the groom a ring? Traditionalists say no. Many modern Jews say yes. Extremely Reform Jews have suggested that the groom might prefer cuff links or a Swiss Army knife.

Step 8: The Reading of the Marriage Contract *(Ketubbah)*. The rabbi reads the marital contract, or *ketubbah*, aloud, commenting as he makes his way through it, "Hmm . . . I personally would never have agreed to that."

THE EXTREMELY REFORM *KETUBBAH*

Since biblical times, Jews have signed *ketubbot* or marriage contracts providing for everything from dowries to what happened if a Jewish wife were kidnapped by a hostile tribe. The contemporary, Extremely Reform *ketubbah* addresses more relevant issues, such as who gets the first shower in the morning. The *ketubbah* is usually inscribed by a skilled calligrapher, and its beauty is such that wedding participants are often heard to gasp, "Nice handwriting!" Though seemingly anachronistic, a well-drafted *ketubbah* can come in handy, e.g. if accused of snoring, you can point out that your *ketubbah* gives you snoring rights. You may even be able to say, "I am snoring on advice of counsel."

Traditional *Ketubbah*	Extremely Reform *Ketubbah*
Must be signed by two witnesses.	Must be signed by two Jehovah's Witnesses.
Husband receives right to generous dowry from wife's family.	No dowry. Husband receives right to hold TV remote control wand.
Husband promises to house, clothe, and feed wife and family.	Husband promises to be sensitive to the problem of sexual harassment in the workplace.
Husband agrees to care for wife if she falls ill.	Husband and wife give each other copies of *Final Exit*.
Husband is assured that wife is a virgin.	Husband and wife assure each other they have no pesky, incurable sexually transmitted diseases.
Husband agrees to cohabit with wife.	Husband and wife agree not to fart in bed.
Husband agrees to do anything to free wife if she is ever taken captive by enemy tribe.	Husband and wife agree never to trade arms for hostages.
Husband agrees that, if there is ever a divorce, he will pay wife 200 *zuzim* (roughly the value of 100 goats).	Husband and wife agree that if there is ever a divorce, it will be really messy.

Step 9: The Recitation of the Seven Marriage Blessings. It is no coincidence that there are seven marriage blessings. During the wedding service, the bride is supposed to circle the groom seven times. There are also seven Torah readings on the Sabbath, and Jewish mystics have noted that there are precisely seven appearances in the Bible of the phrase "when a man takes a wife." Extremely Reform mystics have further noted that there are Seven Dwarves (Happy, Dopey, Grumpy, Bashful, Sleepy, Sneezy, and Doc) and seven members of the Magnificent Seven (Yul Brynner, Steve McQueen, Robert Vaughn, Brad Dexter, James Coburn, Charles Bronson, and Horst Buchholz), and their names may be recited at the Extremely Reform Wedding Ceremony.

WEDGING DANCES	
Traditional	**Extremely Reform**
Mitzvah Tanz (Orthodox men and women dance, but must not physically touch each other.)	*Lambada Tanz* (Extremely Reform men and women must physically touch each other, but not dance.)

Step 10: The Crushing of the Wineglass. The groom stomps on a wineglass, while the rabbi recites the traditional prayer, *"You break it, you pay for it."* It is traditionally said that the smashing of the glass signifies the destruction of the Jewish Temple in Jerusalem ages ago. Anthropologists now theorize that it actually symbolizes the bride's loss of virginity. "But that was also ages ago," you may point out. Below are the other leading explanations of this curious practice.

WHY A WINEGLASS IS CRUSHED AT A WEDDING

1. Crushing a wineglass signifies that a broken marriage is not easily repaired.
2. Crushing a wineglass signifies that a broken wineglass is not easily repaired.
3. Crushing a wineglass signifies that the couple has registered for new wineglasses.
4. Crushing a wineglass signifies that the ceremony is over and that it is time for a Food Fight.

Step 11: The Bride and Groom Leave the *Huppah* to Joyous Recessional Music. The wedding ceremony is over. The guests may now proceed to the Extremely Reform Wedding Reception and enjoy the customary "Serving of the Shellfish Appetizers" and the traditional "Hijacking of the Festivities by the Overbearing Bandleader."

Death and the Extremely Reform Afterlife. Jewish death works something like this: (1) Upon your demise, your soul is separated from your body for faster processing; (2) On the Day of Judgment, your soul is reunited with your body and you are placed in a police lineup; (3) Together, your soul and your body are subjected to yelling and finger-pointing by people you had completely forgotten about.

FUNERALS	
Traditional	**Extremely Reform**
Deceased is wrapped in shroud.	Deceased is wrapped in Shroud of Turin.

QUESTIONS EXTREMELY REFORM JEWS FREQUENTLY ASK ABOUT DEATH

1. I am very worried about what sort of body I will receive when my soul is reunited with my body on the Day of Judgment. What will I look like? Will I be young or old? Also, if, for the sake of argument, I were to die in a trash compactor accident, would I have to spend eternity as a midget?

    Answer: The afterlife is a great mystery. It is believed that most people will be satisfied with the bodies they get back on the Day of Judgment. However, watching over all your body parts is not easy and the Creator cannot be held responsible for keeping track of every single stupid unauthorized change you may have made, especially hair transplants. Stay away from dangerous machinery and try not to get vaporized.

2. I am considering either having my body frozen and stored at a life-extension facility after my death or spending the money on a luxury automobile. What should I do?

    Answer: Buying a new car is always a difficult decision. Have you checked Consumer Reports?

3. If I am a good person, will God reward me, or is life just a cruel riddle, like when an Olympic figure skater trains for fifteen years, then falls down on a triple lutz in the medal round and ends up in fourteenth place with no chance of getting any major advertising contracts?

    Answer: Life is not a cruel riddle. Life is a great mystery.

4. What is my soul doing during the whole time it waits to be reunited with my body?

    Answer: Until the Day of Judgment, your soul is in a state of suspended animation, similar to "escrow."

5. What is "escrow"?

    Answer: Escrow is a great mystery.

EPILOGUE:
THE FUTURE OF
EXTREMELY REFORM JUDAISM

Some Unanswered Questions. Like all Jewish denominations, Extremely Reform Judaism will have to find solutions to difficult problems in the years ahead. Consider that synagogue membership is down, intermarriage is up, and as many as one-quarter of the members of New Age cults are lapsed Jews. Can these trends be sustained? On a slightly different subject, is "Frankenstein" a Jewish name? Also, what religion is Bob Dylan right now? Jewish? Born-Again? Jewish-Again? Who can keep track of these things? For some questions, there are simply no easy answers.

Will Judaism Survive Another 4,000 Years, or Should We Make Other Plans? At present, the Jewish community is divided into two camps: Pessimists, who feel that Judaism is hurtling into oblivion, and Optimists, who feel that things could be getting worse much faster than they are. The Pessimists tend to blame everything on the Extremely Reform Jews, while the Optimists insist that there are many, many invisible signs of

DECLINING JEWISH RELIGIOSITY	
Traditional Jews	**Extremely Reform Jews**
Fear losing followers to ever more reform movements.	Fear losing followers to the Psychic Friends Network.

"Our sins are grievous and the God of Israel is wroth against us. The great Jewish delicatessens goeth downhill and are frequented not by the old regulars. The Catskills lie forsaken and desolate, except for 'singles weekends' at the Concord, which the Almighty findeth disgusting. The people shunneth or eateth most sparingly of the Hebrew National Salami, for, speaking candidly, who needs all that fat and sodium? The old dwelling places of the Lower East Side of New York are become the habitation of bizarre performance artists, yet South Beach in Miami hath gotten too trendy to retire to and play shuffleboard. And people wonder why I'm depressed."

—The Extremely Reform Lamentations of Jeremiah

UNFLAGGING VIGILANCE AGAINST ANTI-SEMITISM

Traditional Jews	Extremely Reform Jews
Always very alert to the slightest signs of resurgent hostility to Jews.	Constantly distracted by amazing scandals involving television evangelists.

Jewish vitality, a theory they keep trying to prove by pointing vaguely into the distance and saying, "See, over there!"

Pessimists also warn that Judaism is in constant danger from renewed anti-Semitism, and that any apparent lull in anti-Semitism is dangerous because it creates the danger of a false lack of danger. Optimists counter that it is dangerous to worry too much about the lack of danger, which they are well aware may be false. This position is disturbing to Pessimists, who then worry about the danger of not worrying about the danger of not worrying about the lack of danger.

Israel, the Ever-Whining People. To keep this debate in perspective, it is worth noting that Judaism has survived countless predictions of its demise. In every age, Jewish elders have complained that the succeeding generation could not possibly carry on their legacy. In every age, Jewish elders have grumbled that this problem would not be so serious if only the succeeding generation would take better notes.

It should also be mentioned that Jews are not the only ones trying to cope with generational change. Islamic fundamentalists worry whether the car bombs of future generations will be as explosive as those that have been detonated in the past. A new generation of Catholics has requested an end to priestly celibacy, while the old-guard church hierarchy responds, "What? Now that we're all seventy years old? Forget it." WASPs at restricted country clubs bellyache that all the good members resign the minute they are nominated to a position in the White House. Many Hare Krishnas are very upset about the deteriorating state of the nation's airports.

Brave New Judaism. Extremely Reform Jews are not backsliding. If asked, many will explain that they are simply searching for different ways to express their Jewishness, preferably ways that are more non-synagogue-centered, non-prayer-oriented, non-participatory, non-content-based, and faith-free. On specific issues, such as the kosher dietary laws, a number of Extremely Reform Jews have even said they would be willing to try to follow them, provided that there were fewer rules about pork and shellfish and more warnings about the dangers of undercooked chicken.

Where all of this will lead is not entirely clear, but a few tentative predictions are attempted below. Meanwhile, the most important thing is for all Jews to try not to lose their Jewish consciousness. Extremely Reform Jews must do what they can to avoid losing consciousness altogether.

SOME EXTREMELY REFORM PREDICTIONS

- Within just a few decades, the problem of the decline in Jewish population will be solved by cloning existing Extremely Reform Jews. This will be a success, as long as they all remember to wear name tags.
- The fierce debate over the definition of "Who is a Jew" will end when rabbis agree to count anyone who is "Jewish-by-birth," "Jewish-by-conversion," or "Jewish-by-process-of-elimination."
- Jewish alienation and self-hatred will vanish, and an Extremely Reform author equal in stature to Philip Roth will write a whole novel about how much he likes himself.
- Relying on advanced satellite communications, rabbis will offer to transmit blessings to Extremely Reform Jews, wherever they happen to be, directly through their dental fillings. This offer will be respectfully declined.
- Life will be found on other planets. Extremely Reform Jews will establish space colonies there, adapt to the environment, and assimilate almost completely.
- By the end of the next century, Jews will begin to find Extremely Reform Judaism much too conservative and onerous. They will start a new denomination, Unbelievably Reform Judaism, which will find many followers.

QUIZ

It was Rabbi Hillel who is said to have asked his students the famous questions, "If I am not for myself, who shall be for me? And if I am for myself alone, what am I? And if not now, when?" Any student who answered incorrectly is said to have been either left back a year or forced to attend Rabbi Hillel's summer school.

See if you can answer the following questions. If you get all of them right, you may be an Extremely Reform Jew. If you get all of them wrong, you definitely are.

1. The stars of "Bonanza"—Lorne Greene ("Ben Cartwright") and Michael Landon ("Little Joe")—were actually, in real life, both Jewish. What religion was "Hoss"?

   a. Beats me.

   b. An atheistic disciple of Nietzsche (or was that the guy on "Gunsmoke"?)

   c. Nobody told me there was going to be a quiz.

2. Do Extremely Reform Jews believe that seemingly random occurrences are the result of predestination, free will, or what?

   a. Predestination.

   b. Free will.

   c. What?

3. The term *shekitah* refers to which aspect of the Jewish dietary laws?
   a. That's so easy, I won't even dignify it with an answer.
   b. How to turn leftovers into zesty cold salads?
   c. I'm sorry, I don't speak Portuguese.

4. A *shulklapper* is a wooden mallet used in the Middle Ages to bang on doors to remind people to come to synagogue. Did you know that?
   a. No, I didn't.
   b. Yes, amazingly, I did.
   c. Why ask questions if you're going to give away the answers beforehand?

5. To Extremely Reform Jews, the word *goyim* means:
   a. Any non-Jewish people.
   b. Christian people.
   c. In-laws.

6. (True or False) The biblical name "Hannah" is, remarkably, spelled the same way forward and backward.
   a. True.
   b. False.
   c. I'd like more time to think.

7. Which of the following is *not* an event at the Maccabiah Games?
   a. The javelin toss.
   b. The discus throw.
   c. Gin rummy.

8. When an infamous Jewish person, such as the late Roy Cohn, is mentioned in conversation in an unflattering way, the appropriate Extremely Reform response is to:

   a. Insist that Roy Cohn was an embarrassment to you, personally, as a Jew, and insist on apologizing profusely on behalf of the entire Jewish people.

   b. Insist that Roy Cohn was not really such a bad guy once you got to know him.

   c. Insist that Roy Cohn was actually Amish.

9. Which of the following is *not* one of the tribes the Israelites did battle with according to the Bible?

   a. The Amalekites.

   b. The Jebusites.

   c. The Transvestites.

10. (Reading Comprehension) Read the passage below and answer the question that follows.

A DUMPLING FOR YOSSEL

Friday was Yossel's favorite day, for on this day the house was filled with wonderful sounds. *Chop-chop* went the knife as Mommy chopped the fish. *Slice-slice* went the carrot peeler as Mommy peeled the carrots. *Floop-floop* went the dumplings as Mommy dropped them into the chicken broth. *Splash-splash* went the water in the bathtub as Yossel scrubbed himself for the special Sabbath meal.

That night, at the dinner table, Daddy went *grumble-grumble.*

"What is it with Yossel?" Daddy said. "He's thirty-five years old and still he wears knee-socks?"

Shh-shh went Mommy. "Don't be so hard on the boy. Yossel, how is your dumpling?"

Yum-yum went Yossel. Because it was.

Question:

Yossel is wearing knee-socks because:

a. Yossel is cold.

b. Yossel is making a fashion statement.

c. It's a free country, isn't it?

11. Match each quotation in column I with its source in column II.

I.	II.
a. "Give me my pound of flesh! No, on second thought, make that a pound of herring salad and some pumpernickel."	1. *The Extremely Reform Dead Sea Scrolls*
b. "Copy this scroll by hand and mail it to ten friends, telling each of them to do exactly as you have done. If you disobey these instructions, you will have a really bad day."	2. *The Extremely Reform Wisdom of King Solomon* 3. *The Extremely Reform Merchant of Venice*
c. "Madam, your objection is overruled. I said, 'Cut the baby in half,' and I meant it. Case closed."	

12. An old Jewish proverb states: "No answer is also an answer." What this really means is:

a. It is O.K. to admit you don't know something.

b. It is O.K. to refuse to answer a question.

c.

13. Which of the following is a widely accepted synonym for Extremely Reform Judaism?

a. Terribly Unorthodox Judaism.

b. I-Can't-Believe-It's-Judaism!™

c. Shmoodaism.